NO WOMAN NO CRY

Rita Marley *with* *Hettie Jones*

NO WOMAN NO CRY

My Life with Bob Marley

HYPERION NEW YORK

CONTENTS

I remember when we used to sit
in the government yard in Trenchtown . . .

In this bright future, you can't forget your past . . .

Oh, little darling . . . oh my little sister . . .
don't shed no tears . . .

No woman, no cry

BOB MARLEY

NO WOMAN NO CRY

PROLOGUE

PEOPLE ASK WHAT it's like when I'm somewhere and suddenly Bob's voice comes on the radio. But the thing about Bob is so deep, it is as if he's always with me, there's always something to remind me. So I don't wait for his voice.

And he did promise me, before he finally closed his eyes, that he'd be here. It was May 11, 1981, and the doctors said he was dying of cancer and that there was no hope. But Bob was hanging on, he wouldn't let go.

I had put his head in my arm, and I was singing "God Will Take Care of You." But then I started to cry and said, "Bob, please, don't leave me."

And he looked up and said, "Leave you, go where? What are you crying for? Forget crying, Rita! Just keep singing. Sing! Sing!"

So I kept singing, and then I realized, wow, that's exactly what the song was saying: "I will never leave you, wherever you are I will be . . ."

So if I hear his voice now, it's only confirming that he's always around, everywhere. Because you do really hear his voice wherever you go. All over the world.

And one interesting thing about it, to me, is that most people only hear *him*. But I hear more, because I'm on almost all of the songs. So I also hear *my* voice, I also hear *me*.

chapter one
TRENCH TOWN ROCK

I WAS AN AMBITIOUS girl child. I knew even then that I had to be, in that environment of thugs, thieves, killers, prostitutes, gamblers—you name it, you'd find it in Trench Town. But alongside the bad lived the good, a lot of strong, talented people who were really aiming at being someone. Barbers. Bus drivers. Seamstresses. Bob himself worked as a welder for a while.

I grew up in the care of my father, Leroy Anderson, a musician who worked as a carpenter. Sometimes I'd go with him to his carpentry jobs, or to hear him play his tenor saxophone. In his woodworking shop outside our house, he'd sit me on the end of the board and call me pet names, like "Colitos," or "Sunshine," or other variations on my full name, Alfarita Constantia Anderson. Because I was very dark-skinned, the kids in school called me "blackie tootus" (black and shiny, with very white teeth). I learned discrimination early and underestimated my own value because of my color. Jamaica has a long history of color consciousness and racial struggle. It's like that old American song, "If you're black, get back, if you're brown, stick around . . ."

Trench Town was, and still is, a ghetto in Kingston, Jamaica's capital. Back then it was a shantytown on tracks and dirt roads. Most people just captured a piece of land, got a government lease for it, and then built anything they could. You'd find cardboard houses, houses made of corrugated metal, concrete block houses. It was like Africa, one hut here, one there. Many places in Jamaica are still like that.

When I was five, my mother, Cynthia "Beda" Jarrett, left Papa and my brother Wesley and me to start a new family with another man. (She kept my other brother, Donovan, who was lighter-skinned.) I loved my mother, because when people would look at us kids and say, "Who fe one is this?" and "Who fe one is that?" I'd always hear, "Oh that's Beda's child" or "Beda's only daughter" and "What a way she grow up fine, sweet little girl!"

But I had been sharing houses out between my mother and her own mother, my grandmother Yaya, before my father decided this was foolishness. Maybe he was jealous of Beda courting another man and felt that we shouldn't be around him. Anyway, I spent more time with Yaya, because I was her complexion—my mother's family is Cuban—and we got along fine. I didn't even mind smelling her cigars—she smoked them backward, with the fire end in her mouth! Yaya's yard was full of her grandchildren, offspring of five daughters, all of whom needed "all-day children stay with you." Yaya was security, she boiled a big pot of cornmeal porridge for the morning serve, and my cousins and I, ages four and five and six, all drank our porridge and ate our crackers and then went off to our little prep school.

When my father decided that he would rather have us living with him, he asked his sister Viola if she would help. Viola had no children, but she was married and trying to build her own life, and didn't feel she had to do this. Until our grandparents, who were fond of us, intervened and urged her to consider it. "You must help Roy," our grandfather is supposed to have said, "because these are good children and need your help." This grandfather, a tailor, died just about the same time as Aunty Viola Anderson Britton agreed to take us into her house. So I didn't get a chance to know him, but I've got a lot to thank him for. I wouldn't say I've lost anything by not going with my mother; I think I've grown into the woman that I ought to be by being raised by my aunty and my father and my brother, because they all played a part. We had to support each other.

Aunty was first of all a dressmaker and designer of wedding clothes, in partnership with her sister, Dorothy "Tita" Walker, whom we kids called "Fat Aunty." All over Kingston people knew that if you wanted a wedding, all the way from the bride and groom to the page boy, "The Two Sisters" were the ones to see. Their specialty was wedding dresses with bridesmaid and flower girl. And don't forget the cake—Aunty could make that too—from one to five layers! For a time she also kept a cold supper shop in the lane outside our house, where we sold ginger beer, pudding, fish, fried dumplings, tea, soup. All to make a living. Her husband, Herman Britton, was a driver for Public Works. He was very good to me, and I thought of him as my stepfather, but he and Aunty had problems and would fuss when he came home drunk every Friday night. Apart from that, he was a quiet, peaceful man. Mr. Britton had two sons outside the marriage, and eventually he and Aunty divorced.

I don't know how she managed it, but 18A Greenwich Park Road, where we lived, was one of the best-looking houses around. It had started as a "government house," a wooden structure with a zinc (tin) roof, part of a government housing scheme. Now it had three bedrooms, a sewing room, an outside kitchen and pit toilet, a veranda, and a fence with a gate you could lock, which was very unusual in Trench Town, where in those days every place was open and you could walk into anyone's yard. We also had radio and later television, and even water piped into our yard, so we didn't have to go to the standpipe to catch water like most people who lived there.

Though we all had our chores, Aunty always employed one or two helpers to tend to the housework while she sewed. Mas King was our hand helper. He would work with Aunty to add on to the house, or to lay down the zincs when they would lift up off the roof in a high wind or heavy rain. But she'd always be the one in charge—Mas King would be down below reaching the nail and she up there hammering! Aunty was a go-getter with a flair, a special character. She was a small woman, but energetic and intense, feisty—in Jamaica we pronounce that *face-ty*. Aunty could definitely get in your face. She was still in her early thirties when I went to live with her, very pretty and sexy. Long as I knew her she maintained her good body and beautiful skin. But she was way more than appearance—I used to call her the village lawyer, because she was into *everything*. Everybody come complain to Miz Britton, so and so and so, and if anything happened in the area they'd rush to tell her. She also ran "partner," a lottery where everyone gave her money and then got to draw at the end of the week. She was a breadwinner for the community and very "government," making sure everyone voted, and if anything happened—like I said, she was in *charge*. I know it was no small thing for a woman like that to take in two young children, but I think she did it with an open heart, because she loved her brother and respected her parents. And in return she was well loved, always loved. More than loved, our *beloved* Aunty.

Papa used to make stools on his carpentry bench outside our home, and I had one for myself. Everyone knew this was Colitos's stool, sort of benchy with four legs and a square top, but very neatly done with a finish. So you could know that someone had a father who is a fine carpenter here. I sat on it during my break time or if I wanted to stay by Aunty's machine while she sewed, cleaning up something or pulling out stitches or just watching and learning. Eventually I became a hemmer for her, hemming skirt tails and all of that.

Aunty's nickname was "Vie" (pronounced *vye*), and I had my own sweet name for her—"Vie Vie." Whenever I said "Vie Vie," things would work out. But whenever she spanked me I'd think, oh why did she? If she loved me so much she wouldn't spank me! Oh it's because she's only my Aunty, oh how I wish I could be with my mother! Many times after I was spanked I would take my stool to the house corner and sit down and cry. I can see myself now, looking left and then right to see if I was alone, because if the helpers or anyone else saw me crying they would tell—"Rita out there cry, ma'am!" So I would cry secretly, wondering why, why did she have to hit me? Is it because I don't have a mother? Is it because I don't have any mother . . . And then I would bawl, really bawl good and loud, to make sure she came out there and saw me and heard what I said. Because she didn't feel as if I needed a mother besides her.

And gradually, when I visited my mother's house and had to sleep with about fifteen other cousins and had to carry this and that and sweep up, and didn't get much attention, I began to understand and be grateful that this was not my home. Aunty's, where my room was, where I was cared for, was *home* and where I belonged.

When I was nine my mother got married and didn't invite me to the wedding. That hurts, when you're a little girl. I didn't want Aunty to know how hurt I felt, I felt I couldn't let her know, especially since she'd always said, "Your mother don't know you're a girl child, she won't even send you a panty." Which, of course, had led me to think that my mother just didn't care and could have left me feeling lost.

But Aunty was way ahead of me. "You don't even have to hurt," she said in her no-nonsense way. "Your mother don't want to invite you? No problem! I will make you a beautiful dress, and I'll dress you up, and we'll pass by the wedding, and just let everyone see how pretty you are and see what your mother did—wu'thless bitch!"

That's how Aunty was, she could be very mean when she felt it was necessary. But she had standards—yes, quality—so much class! And she was so righteous! And for this I came to appreciate her, to understand why

I *should* love her and not let anything be too good for her. Wesley and I, when we got old enough, we'd say to our father, there were times we didn't even know where you were, but Aunty was always there for us. You look up, you think there's no one, and here comes Aunty.

The Andersons were a musical family. Besides my father and Aunty (who sang in her church choir), I was close to my Uncle Cleveland, a big baritone very much in demand for weddings and other celebrations. So I was always musically oriented, musically inclined. And because it was recognized so early that I had a voice, Aunty would teach me songs and then tell her customers, "Oh Rita could sing the wedding song." I loved singing in church, too—I'm a true Christian from when I was a child. I know there is a God; I love Him and have always felt very close to Him. (And then there was the pastor's son, Winston, who would walk me home after church and kiss me at the gate.)

Saturday afternoons on RJR, one of the two Jamaica radio stations, there was a program called *Opportunity Knocks*. If you got on it, you would be exposed to people who could take you from nowhere (like Trench Town) and put you into helpful organizations like the Girl Guides. Or they'd give you a bit of cash and a trip somewhere. I was ten when Aunty said, "You want to try for the radio, Rita?" Aunty, she was oh so confident in me! So I said, "Okay, what am I gonna sing?" And she said, "The Lord's Prayer, because that's a *big* tune, and you can *do* it!"

She sat me down on my little stool, beside her sewing machine, and day after day she'd be there sewing and singing "Our father" and I'd repeat "Our father." "Who art in heaven . . ." "Thy kingdom come . . ." And when we reached the last of it, she'd say, "And now we put our hands together like this: 'And the glllooooorrry . . .'"

The night of the program she dressed me up in a crinoline and a fabulous blue skirt and blouse with lace trim. I was way too short for the microphone and they had to put me on a box, but *oh*, I tore that place down! All

I can remember is, "And tonight's talented winner is . . . Rita Anderson!" And everyone yelling, "You won! Rita, you won!"

I went up on the stage and for the first time experienced the applause of an audience. I was so little, but I think of her, that little girl—myself—as so courageous! And from that day on, I said, hey, I'm gonna be a singer.

Often the only way to keep a Jamaican family surviving was—and still is—for one of its members to emigrate and send money home. The way people go to New York now, in that time our refuge was England. You went by boat, and the fare was very cheap, seventy-five pounds. Though it might take people years to save that up, eventually the recommendation was, "If you're gonna tu'n wu'thless, g'wan to England and find a job." When I was thirteen, Aunty said to my father, "You're getting nowhere. Where's your ambition? You can't stay in Jamaica sawing wood and playing saxophone twice a week. Rita's turning teenager—I'll soon have to buy her brassieres!" She bought Papa a ticket to England and said, "Go find a life." So, like others, he went to London. He used his carpentry skills and drove taxis but managed still to work as a musician, playing his tenor sax and living in various European cities.

Wesley and I had thought that when Papa went to England we were going to be following him in a year or two. That was always a promise: If you behave yourself, you will go to your father. If you behave yourself . . . And so I was always looking forward to that and hoping to one day tell my friends, "I'm going to England 'cause that's where my father is, my Papa's sending for me." But that dream never materialized because he was never financially able. Although he kept in touch, I didn't see him for more than ten years; in fact, Bob saw him before I did! This is why Aunty meant so much, because she gave me the reason to be a tower of strength. She gave me that ambitious feeling. She'd say, "Just because your mother left you and your father's gone doesn't mean you'll be nobody. I'm Aunty. You're going to be someone."

9

· · ·

Across the street from our house, on the opposite side of Greenwich Park Road, the Calvary Cemetery held most of Trench Town's Catholic dead. Though it wasn't something we had any fear of, living in front of a cemetery was an experience. We were always being faced with life and death, because every day there were three or four bodies and at least one elaborate funeral with beautiful flowers and ribbons. Our neighbor Tata was the caretaker there, and his wife, Mother Rose, was Aunty's best friend. So we had access to the cemetery anytime, and were able to squeeze ourselves through the barbed wire or even go through the gate if we wanted. And since Tata knew I needed ribbons for school and that Aunty and I loved flowers, if there was a special funeral that came in, he would send someone to tell us, and after the mourners left, I climbed in. Other kids said, "You don't afraid?" At school they would tease me that my hair ribbon was from a funeral. Or they'd say, "Oh no, you have to come through the cemetery to get to school! I'm afraid of you, girl!" But then there were my friends who would fight for me, who said, "Foolish! You stupid! So what? She's intelligent, she can *sing*!!"

It was our family's custom to gather every evening and sing, under the plum tree in the yard—the "government yard" that Bob would later so famously sing about. From the time I was small, the yard had been my special place, not only where I cried after Aunty's spankings, but where I went just to be by myself and think. It was smooth dirt, swept clean (often by me), and the plum tree had beautiful yellow blossoms. I used to pick the plums when they were green and gummy inside and break them in half and stick them on my ears, to make *fabulous* plum earrings.

When I was fourteen, Fat Aunty died, and her son, my eleven-year-old cousin Constantine "Dream" Walker, came to live with us. Since they'd lived only one street away, he and I had always been close, and because of the "Two Sisters" business we'd grown up more like brother and sister than cousins. Aunty had taught us harmony, and so Dream became my harmonizer, pretending to be the band. Evenings, in the yard, he and I performed together. Every song that played on the radio, we had it down pat. We listened to Miami stations that played rhythm and blues, singers like Otis Redding and Sam Cooke and Wilson Pickett and Tina Turner, and groups like the Impressions, the Drifters, the Supremes, Patti LaBelle and the Bluebells, the Temptations—we caught all the Motown hits. But if you lived in Trench Town then, you'd also hear "ska," and even earlier kinds of music like Nyahbingi drumming and "mento," with roots in African traditions—the way in the States you might hear soul and pop on the radio but also folk and blues from way back.

Sometimes Dream and I would put on a show and draw a crowd, charging people half a penny apiece. The people in the community, neighbors, other kids, the good, the bad—everyone looked forward to our "special entertainment" evenings. Even some of Papa's musician friends came to hear us, people like Roland Alphonso and Jah Jerry. With Papa's help, we'd made "pan guitars" from sardine cans. First, he nailed a flat piece of wood to the can for the fret board, and then we fixed strings onto it. Our "guitars" were small, but they worked!

At my school, the Central Branch government school on Slipe Pen Road, my name had been shortened from Alfarita to Rita because the teacher said it was too long for the register. At Central Branch nothing was something; we wore white blouses, blue pleated skirts, and blue ties, and considered ourselves fortunate. I don't know how Aunty had even gotten me in there, because you were supposed to live in the area in the first place, as well as having a good family background and somebody or some school to recommend you. I was kind of far from all that, living in Trench Town with no mother and Papa being a carpenter and a musician with no established earnings. I think Aunty surely must have pulled some strings; probably she got a letter from some member of her political party, as she was the area representative. But I showed myself deserving of the chance. I always loved school, was always "a bright girl," as my teachers said, not always by the book but by my common sense and quick pickup of the lessons. Except math. I tried my best and was very good at everything else.

Lunchtime, in elementary schools, different vocal groups gathered in classrooms to compete. At Central Branch I was one of the organizers, and if there was to be a concert—often just before a holiday—Mrs. Jones, my favorite teacher, would say, "Rita, we need some songs," and she'd make sure I had time and space for rehearsals. I'd tell everyone in my group what to do, what parts to sing and when. And all the while I'm telling myself that one day I'll be like Diana Ross.

In Jamaica, public education is free only through elementary school, and then you need money. After Central Branch I got a half scholarship to Dunrobin High School (Merle Grove Extension)—meaning that the government would pay half and the rest was up to the family—and I had just Aunty and my brother Wesley to support me. We had problems after a while keeping up with lunch money, books, and all the fees for this and that, until Wesley, who at the time was going to Walgrove College, decided to get a day job and pick up his own lessons in the evening. What a brother. He and Aunty were always behind me, convinced that I was to be someone, that there was something in me that promised this (even though Aunty doubted it more than once when my math grades were not what she wanted).

Wesley was the kind of guy who was always in school, but by the time I was seventeen I wanted to be able to get a job as fast as I could, so that I could take care of myself and stop depending on his income. And I felt I couldn't continue to just live off Aunty. I didn't have anything in mind about being a singer—in Jamaica you have to be realistic if you want to have any kind of a life. So when I left high school I went straight to the Bethesda School of Practical Nursing. And because the best recommendation for striving young girls was to get a secretarial job, I enrolled in night school at Papine to learn shorthand and typing. I had a boyfriend by this time, one of a pair of twins, who also liked to sing and with his brother was trying to create a Jamaican version of Sam and Dave. Evenings, after he left his job, he'd come for me at school and we would slowly, lovingly, make our way home.

And so, like many other girls of that age, I got sidetracked. I was waiting to start work in one of the big hospitals in Kingston, where you had to be at least eighteen, when I got pregnant. Teenage sex was such a shame when I was growing up, at least in Aunty's opinion. I didn't dare tell her, but morning sickness exposed me. "Why you spittin'?" she demanded. And eventually I had to confess.

This was one of the greatest sins I could have committed while under Aunty's watchful eye. Everyone was disappointed in me. "Let's take her to the doctor and get rid of it," was the general recommendation. "Oh no, you can't have it," said the boy's mother. "He's too young, and you're too young. You would never make it, you both need to go back to school." She sent him to England, although he went unwillingly, because we were in love and he had been looking forward to being a father. After he left I decided to have the baby anyway, even though Aunty insisted that if anyone came to the house I was to get under the bed or stay behind the door.

I was frightened but brave when I gave birth at Jubilee Hospital to my first child, a girl I named Sharon. And it didn't surprise me that after she was born she became Aunty's child, the belle of the ball. As for me, my nineteenth birthday found me out of school and still waiting for that nursing job in the hospital.

Sharon's birth didn't change our home life much. Dream and I continued to get together to practice songs we'd heard on the radio; evenings we sang under the plum tree in the yard. Often he and I were joined by Marlene "Precious" Gifford, a girlfriend of mine who was still in high school, who would come by to play with the baby and fill me in on the latest gossip and keep me up to date on what was happening. She had a good voice, and with Dream we made a fine trio. One day, while we were rehearsing for one of our yard shows, I said to them, "You know, we could form a group." It seemed as if everybody in Trench Town tried to sing or play an instrument or get a vocal group together.

At that time, the mid-sixties, everybody I knew was excited about a new Jamaican music known as "rock steady." Our favorite stars were Toots and the Maytals, Delroy Wilson, the Paragons, Ken Booth, Marcia Griffiths, and particularly a group who called themselves the Wailing Wailers. The Wailers had recorded some rock steady singles in a studio in the Trench Town area near where Dream and I lived. Kingston had a number of small recording studios then, some of them just one of several businesses run by one person—Beverley's Record and Ice Cream Parlor was one (its owner also sold stationery); another was a combination studio and liquor store. Studio One, on Brentford Road, belonged to "Sir Coxsone," a man named Clement Dodd, who was an early supporter of Jamaican music and very important to its progress.

When I found out that the Wailing Wailers passed our house every day on their way to Coxsone's studio, I told Dream and Marlene that we ought to meet them and sing for them. One evening when I looked out they were passing the cemetery, so the three of us ran out to wave. Looking at them— there were three of them, too—I thought, well, they look all right, I could be friends with those guys. Even though Aunty was always saying, "Don't look out for that boy business, you already have one baby, so just be cool now, you're either going to work or back to school or I'll have to send you to your father—you're not going to stay here and be an inconvenience!"

Nevertheless, I began to watch for the Wailers and listen to them on the radio, and one day not long afterward they stopped and waved back, and Peter Tosh, the tall one, came across the street while the two others leaned on the cemetery wall, strumming their guitars. Peter introduced himself—his real name was Winston Hubert McIntosh—and asked me how I was, and what was my name, and called me a "nice girl."

"So you're the Wailers," I said. "And who's that one?"

"That's Bunny," he said. "And the other is Robbie."

"Hi!" I yelled across the street, all the while trying to think of a way to tell them that we could sing. Later I said to Dream, "Let's try to practice that song 'What's Your Name?' by Sam and Dave."

The next time the Wailers came past and stopped to greet us, I said to Peter, "You know, we can sing a bit."

And he said, "Well sing then, man."

Aunty had been so strict with me since I'd had Sharon that I hadn't even been allowed to talk to boys out of our yard. "Don't make me feel like I'm an old woman just because I have a baby! I'm still young, I still can be happy!" I had yelled at her. But the rule was that I could only socialize over the fence, so when Peter asked, I opened the gate and stood half in and half out. And we sang.

The next day not just Peter but the one called Robbie came over. This time I was alone. He and I said hello, but he was shy, and I thought, oh, nice boy. Then Peter said, "You look like a decent girl, and it seems as if you can sing, so why don't you let us take you up to Coxsone's for an audition one of these days?"

That was an offer I needed to consider. Would those guys take me away and rape me? After all, Trench Town was full of risky, tough "rude boys," and most of them could sing.

By then, though, a few of Papa's friends were aware of our talent after having heard Dream and me in the yard. Andy Anderson and Denzil Lang were also friends of Coxsone, so one day they decided to pull some strings and take us up to see him.

All excited but a little nervous, Marlene, Dream, and I went to the studio—and there were the Wailing Wailers, who were surprised now as well as interested. It was great—we did a few songs, and then Coxsone asked Robbie to play the guitar for us while we sang some more.

I could tell it was important to all three of the Wailers to see that

Dream and I were being raised strictly, that we had discipline from our house, that we had been brought to Coxsone by older men who knew music. Robbie in particular seemed to take that as something very positive. And I think he started to feel interested in me then. But that first day I was just freelancing, I wasn't really concentrating on any special one of them. It was exciting enough just to be at Coxsone's, where you see people you hear on the radio!

Did I have any idea that in a few short months this Robbie Marley, the shy guitarist, would become the love of my life? Did I suspect that he'd become a major force, world-renowned, an icon of musical history?

No! What was on my mind was Aunty's warning: "Don't you dare stay too long because you have to give the baby titty when she wakes up!!"

S TUDIO ONE HAD probably been a home before Coxsone bought it. He had taken down walls, but it was easy to imagine where the bedroom used to be and the kitchen and the hall. So you felt like you were at home there, because it was less like a business and more like a family affair. When anything happened, everybody got excited—the musicians, the singers, the man outside. And the hype was, "We do a hit tune today." "We" meaning it was everybody's hit tune. We would be there for days, nights, days, but nobody complained—it was just fun to wake up and say, "*Oooh,* I have studio today!"

Coxsone had recorded some of the most successful groups in Jamaica, including the famous "Skatalites," one of the earliest ska bands. (The word "ska" comes from a certain sound made by the electric guitar.) Marcia Griffiths, who later sang with me as one of the I-Three, says that Studio One was Jamaica's Motown, "where all the great stars grew . . . like a university you graduate." A lot of times different people would be working at once; songs were being written in every corner. You couldn't help but learn if you kept your ears open. Coxsone had a guitar that he loaned to those who were too poor to buy one. Bob had that guitar most of the time.

The backup group we eventually formed still consisted of Dream, myself, and Marlene, who would leave school in the evenings to come to Trench Town and rehearse, and whose parents thought this was the worst ambition. To leave high school to go to Trench Town, to be with those kinds of people—the tough guys, the killers, the thieves!

Dream was my main tootsie, my favorite cousin, my little postman, my little errand runner. As a baby, he had the most beautiful big eyes you've ever seen, and always looked as if he was dreaming—you know that sexy dreamy look? So from an early age Constantine Anthony Walker was known as "Dream." He was only about thirteen, the baby amongst us, when we met the Wailers. They, being the Misters of Black Progress, who taught us that Black Is Beautiful and how wise it is to know yourself, decided that Dream was so much their little "buds" (buddy) that they had to change his nickname. Only old men have *dreams*, they insisted, but young men have *visions*. And so Dream became Vision. A much more youthful flavor!

We sang behind the Wailers and sometimes behind other singers or groups who were recording. Coxsone and some others on the scene suggested we name ourselves something like the Marvelettes, an American group we'd heard, and so we became the "Soulettes." Our first big hit, with Delroy Wilson also singing background, was "I Love You, Baby." This was a big, big thrill for us. We were unknown, we weren't out there in the show business arena, and we were all still teenagers, starry-eyed amateurs.

It was also Coxsone's suggestion that Bob train and rehearse us, and I guess by then he must have seen something happening between Bob and me.

He was pretty handsome, I thought—Robert Nesta Marley, Robbie to all of us then. Jamaicans would call him brown-skinned and Americans might say light-skinned. His father, Captain Norval Sinclair Marley, was an older white man, a native Jamaican who had retired from the British Army. Bob had much of his father's imprint; he was very half-black, half-white, with a high, round forehead, prominent cheekbones, and a long nose. His mother, Cedella "Ciddy" Malcolm, was seventeen when she met Norval. He was more than twice her age, and was then the superintendent for British-owned lands in the rural parish of St. Ann, where Ciddy lived. By the time she was nineteen, she'd been seduced by, married to, and then abandoned by Norval. The one time he saw his father, Bob used to say, the old man offered him a "Willy" penny (an old copper coin, thought of as a collector's item). Bob claimed he never saw Norval again.

But like me, Bob had an extended family to raise him, at least for a while. His grandfather, Omeriah Malcolm, was a *myalman*, or healer, as well as a successful businessman respected in his community of Nine Miles. So it didn't surprise me that Bob, as the world would come to know, was very black conscious—his black consciousness covered his light skin. You see him, you hear him, and he's a black man. And he was very disciplined, self-disciplined. Very real.

At fourteen he had come from St. Ann to Kingston with his mother, to live with her and a man named Thaddius (Taddy) Livingston, who had offered her work in his bar. Ciddy had a daughter, Pearl, with Taddy, but then found out he was already married and had other women besides. Looking for a better life, she took Pearl, who was still a baby, and migrated to Wilmington, Delaware, where she had some family and friends. Bob was left in Taddy's care, but more like on his own. He told me that his mother's plan had been to send for him in three months, as soon as she was settled and could secure the necessary papers. But the papers weren't easy to get. The three months had become more than three years.

When we met, Bob was living in an uneasy situation with Taddy Livingston, Taddy's common-law wife, and his son Neville Livingston, called Bunny, the member of the Wailers eventually known as Bunny Wailer. With his mother away, Bob lacked the kind of support and defense I got from Aunty. (One of his early songs is titled "Where Is My Mother.") Taddy's woman resented him, as the son of a woman who had had an affair with her man. One day Bob told me how fed up he was with both Taddy and this "stepmother," who wanted him to be her maid because he wasn't bringing any money to the house. For a while he had simply become an errand boy, then worked as a trainee in a welding shop, before making his first singles, "Judge Not" and then "One Cup of Coffee," on the Beverley's label. That Bob was getting some attention didn't mean he was being paid very much. No one had money then.

At first, and maybe always, I cared for Robbie Marley from a sisterly point of view. I was that sort of person, and still am—the responsible kind. I saw him and I said, "poor thing." It wasn't "I love him," but "poor thing." My heart went out to him. I kept thinking, oh, what a *nice* boy. So nice that I didn't want to let him know I had a baby—in those days, for a teenager to be unmarried and have a baby seemed so shameful. During this time I spent many hours at Studio One, rehearsing and recording, and always managed to conceal that fact. But one day, right in the middle of recording, my breasts started to leak, and Bob noticed. He said, a little surprised, "What's that? You have a baby?" It was not said unkindly.

Although I was terribly embarrassed, I couldn't deny the evidence, so I just nodded.

And he said, "I could tell. Why you didn't let us know? Why you didn't ask to go home early? Is it a boy or girl?"

"Well, it's a girl," I said.

"Where is she? What is her name? Where is her father? Can I see her?"

All these questions came fast, with great concern. I stood there, looking at him, unable to answer right away. I found that concern to be very mature for a young man still in his teens—like caring and at the same time maybe seeing me through a different eye. His interest in my baby made me feel proud instead of ashamed. That to me was a good sign, but so unexpected. Finally he said, "Go home and feed your baby and I'll see you later."

And this is where my love came in. I looked at him and thought, uh-oh, such a *nice* guy. And I got weak in the knees. Oh my God, I thought, oh my God.

That evening, he did come by. Sharon was about five months old then. When I brought her out, he loved her. And she loved him. When she learned to talk a little she couldn't say "Robbie," so she called him "Bahu."

From that day on, when you'd see Bob, I'd be his tail. He'd have me by the hand, walking me, come on, Rita. When all this first started, Sharon's father and I were still corresponding. Bob didn't like that and made his position clear. In fact, he insisted that I end the relationship—why was I having anything to do with a man who wouldn't help me or the baby? One day he caught Dream with a letter to be mailed to Sharon's father and took it away from him! (That ended the correspondence.)

I learned firsthand about his generosity then, this Robbie, the kind of man he was, because whenever he had a little money he'd come by the house with some Cow & Gate baby food and a drink for Aunty. And even she began to give in to his nice ways and manners. "Well," she said, "it looks like something is going on here."

And so, though I didn't expect this, I became *his*. As in okay now, guys, this is *my* girl. Even Peter Tosh respected that and learned not to touch, because Peter was very touchy, he would see you and *ohh*—hug you up and try to squeeze you.

But Bob said, no no no . . . this is *my* girl.

It wasn't long before Coxsone put out a Wailers album with the Soulettes behind them. Released in 1965, it was called *The Wailing Wailers*. Since Dream was so much younger than Marlene and I, and had a soft, sweet voice, our female voices overpowered his presence, and the main impression the Soulettes gave was that of a female group. I was the lead singer, and eventually, when we started to get bookings for concerts, two other young women—Cecile Campbell and Hortense Lewis—came in, as Dream sometimes wasn't able to go on the road, either because he had to go to school or because he was restricted by his age from some of the events that we were allowed to attend.

I loved performing live, under the bright lights and inside the music, being onstage. And it was a thrill to be earning a little money independently. But I still wasn't sure about giving up the security of a nursing career, although I loved music so much and it seemed as if that's what I was going after. Bob and I were always meeting, rehearsing, talking, giving each other advice. One of the important aspects of our relationship was that we were friends before we became lovers, we were naturally friendly, like brother and sister. He was always teaching me to hold notes and other aspects of music. He was *concerned* about me. "You're a *nice* girl," he'd caution, "so don't get mix up, these men will use you and abuse you, and you could be caught up and have many more babies and destroy yourself. So don't follow them, see about your *work*. Decide! Decide whether you really love music or want to go back to nursing, but be serious about whatever you do."

The Jamaican dancehall has been called "nightclub, news medium, gathering place, church, theater, and schoolhouse all rolled into one." Contemporary Jamaican pop music is known as "dancehall." A dance "hall" could actually happen anywhere, indoors or out. Sometimes a crowd got together in a building, but just as often the place would be a yard or a field or a parking lot. There was either live music or a DJ playing records, with the music booming out over a sound system through huge speakers. DJs might talk over the music, like American radio disc jockeys, to crank up the energy and keep people moving. Sometimes two sound systems played against each other at the same dancehall, to see who would attract the larger audience, just as in the States, in New Orleans, jazz bands would have "cutting contests" in the street and try to drown each other out.

Although I had always listened to records and to the radio, because of having been brought up so strictly I hadn't seen much, so I was new to all this excitement. I'd never actually gone to a dancehall until Bob took me. By then the Wailers were one of the top male groups in Jamaica, and their recordings were being played at the dances as well as on the radio. Since their presence at any location always had an impact and could promote record sales, it was recommended that on Friday and Saturday nights the group go to one of the dancehalls. At first Bob didn't even want to take me. He'd say things like, "You know there's a dance tomorrow, but I don't think I should take you because there might break a fight." And I'm saying, "No, I wanna see the fight!"

But apart from the fighting, those first dancehall experiences were to me—whew, astonishing! Watching everybody bumping and grinding— to me that was all new. And of course, just as Bob had predicted, a fight would break out during the dance—that happened regularly in those days. It was the normal thing! We didn't have gun shooting then, but a guy would break a bottle, or would pull out his ratchet knife, and put it to another guy's throat, and say, "I'll kill you if you dance with my girlfriend one more time!"

There were times Bob had to take my hand and pull me out of a crowded area, just to escape the bottle throwing. So he was always saying, "I told you!" at the end of the night. But the scene didn't bother me, because I found it all so exciting—this was the "real world," the world I hadn't been in until I met him.

People have asked me since then whether there were times I had to choose between being with Sharon and being with Bob, something that can happen when you're developing a new relationship and already have a child to be responsible for. But I didn't really have to make that choice. We *both* became parents for Sharon, and I seldom left her behind for long, because Bob was not that type of a daddy. He would make sure to remind me! "Whatever you're doing, hurry up because you have to go home to the baby." Or "You think Aunty can manage until we finish the session?" He was very conscientious, and this was something that impressed me greatly—his sharing, his caring for *my* baby, and really allowing me to show more responsibility. To him I was not just the ordinary girl running around with nothing to do but play and hang out. He'd even chastise me: "You have a baby to look after, now don't stay here and waste time!" Or if the session was running too long he'd say, "Rita, you sure you can stay longer than this? Your baby don't want titty? You don't want to go home and feed the baby and come back?" So he was always there, attentively reminding me, hey, you have a baby . . .

I was now growing up to be what was called then a *nice* young lady. The young man I still knew as Robbie had other girls in his life, girls with whom he had intimate relationships; I knew that he was not a saint. But he kept them away from me out of respect.

The first time we kissed, we actually had a real date. He took me to the Ambassador, our local Trench Town theater, which offered concerts and sometimes live performances as well as movies. The Ambassador was where the people went, where parents took their children, boys met girls, boyfriends met girlfriends. But dating was not on Aunty's list, so I couldn't simply say to Bob, "Okay, I'd like to go to the movies with you." I had to make up some story about a special rehearsal, since she didn't mind my going to rehearsals because she knew and respected the fact that I had that mission, that I was trying to do something. Of course she said okay, but she couldn't help adding, "Be back by eight or nine!"

"Oh, of course," I lied. And then it was off to the movies.

I can't remember the name of the film because after the first few minutes we were only sort of, but not quite, watching it. Most of the time we were looking into each other's eyes, just looking into each other's eyes for a good while—which we had a habit of doing, possibly because of working together and trying to get the music cues right. But the eyes say so much— I used to have to watch Aunty's eyes to take messages, like to go left with a double wink, or right, move fast. It was the same with Bob, our eyes were always our way of communicating, and instead of looking at the screen we were looking into each other's eyes and then we were kissing and I couldn't believe it, I was so blown away! And I could see he was too, totally blown away, but I was in better control and I realized that this could go on to something else that I really couldn't even think about, so don't let's think about it, let's just look at the screen!

Those days when we were courting, Studio One was our commitment; we hardly ever went any place else. We would meet there at nine or ten in the morning if there was an early session, and we'd be there until break time, when we'd get something to eat, like a meat patty, with a coco bread and a bottle of soda—that was the daily food, all we could afford, though occasionally Bob's friends might make porridge or soup (Bunny was a very good cook and made the more daring soup concoctions). Then there were times when we were privileged to be together at concerts. The Soulettes were already a hot female group in Jamaica and the Wailing Wailers the number one male group, with all the girls going crazy over them. And I'm there being Miss Queen, because although all three Wailers made much of me and made me feel special, at the same time I was feeling so sure about Robbie, sure that everybody understood "that one is mine." Though I didn't really have to say it because he would never leave me for a moment.

Among my favorite memories of that time is an event involving Lee "Scratch" Perry, one of the funniest characters to come out of Studio One. Early on, Scratch was the man who did the cleaning up for Coxsone. But like everyone else around the place, if he'd seen any special talent and had an idea that this or that person might make it, he would recommend them. Coxsone was always open to that. Just about the time the Soulettes had begun to think of ourselves as the top background vocalists for the studio, he called us in one day to do some work with Lee Perry.

I said, "Lee Perry! Scratch? But Scratch is like the yard man, you know?"

And Coxsone said, "No man, lately he's been auditioning talents for me, and now he has a hit tune called 'Roast Duck,' and it will need some background vocals."

So I asked Bob what he thought, and he said, "Well, you don't need to do it, but it's not a big thing, if you feel you want to."

And I agreed that I wanted to do it out of gratitude, because Scratch was so nice to us, preparing us for concerts and being the roadie guy. So we gave him that respect and went over to do the sound for him. It worked out just fine and everybody got excited and hey! Scratch's recording came out and it went on the sound systems! Everyone was hyped! Go Perry!

Soon a big stage show was planned at the Ward Theatre and Scratch was to be on it, and he was walking on his head—he couldn't believe that this was happening to him, that his dream, which he'd kept quiet, was happening! The Wailers, the Soulettes, Delroy Wilson, the Paragons—all of Studio One's best-known artists—were performing, and Scratch was to be the opening act.

And so he went onstage first, and as backup we followed him. Scratch started his song, "Me say me wan roast duck," and there we were, on the side, echoing, "We wan roast duck, we wan roast duck." And it was like . . . a comedy! Scratch was that kind of a person anyway, a real comedy, he wore a lot of glass and things on himself, and as he went on singing the audience started to throw things—not stones, luckily—but paper cups! Paper cups rained onto the stage, and then bottles! And I'm saying to myself, now why did we get ourselves into this?

But to us it was fun—fun to see him running off the stage and realizing that it was not his time, just not his time, though he had tried. (His time would come much later, when in 2003 his album *Jamaica E.T.* won a

Grammy Award in the Reggae category.) Back then, though, I respected Coxsone for giving Lee Perry that opportunity, to say to the man, "If you feel you can do it, go do it!" But you also have to see that it takes more than doing it in the studio, that when you go out there and face five hundred or five thousand people you have to deliver—or else they're going to deliver paper cups and bottles! And that was the first—and only—time I've been stoned off the stage.

Clement "Sir Coxsone" Dodd played a great role in Bob's life. It was he who offered that initial encouragement so important to any young musician. Bob told me Coxsone had said to him, "Now, young man, be strong. Think. You can make music. Write. Sing." So even though little or no money was coming in, Bob was getting that crucial support from someone he respected, someone who had the power to help him.

The situation was different where he was living. One day he said to me, "Rita, I can't take this."

I looked at him; he seemed especially tired and very sad. I asked, "Take what?"

He said, "When Mr. Taddy come home in the nights, he wake me up to have his dinner. He don't wake his son up. No matter what time of the morning he comes in, it's 'Nesta, Nesta, wake up, hot up me food.' And I have to serve him his dinner. Be the houseboy the next morning." Taddy's woman had been mistreating him too—"like a little slave boy," Bob said. Because she was still carrying a feud over his mother having had a baby for Taddy.

That night, after we talked about it a while, he decided to leave Taddy's house. He went to Coxsone, whose first response was, "If you feel it's right, Robbie." But then he must have seen how miserable Bob was and how Bob relied on him, because Bob told me Coxsone just smiled then and said, "Well, Robbie, there's the audition room at the back of the studio, you can use it in the night."

So that's how our life together started—from nowhere, from nothing. From the days when Bob was sleeping at Coxsone's, alone, on the floor or on a door. When I thought of him, it was still as *nice boy,* and Coxsone probably saw how much Bob was hanging on to me, too, saying *nice girl* as well. But I think Bob was ahead of me and Coxsone both; I think he was thinking *way* ahead, he wasn't just thinking for a girlfriend, he was thinking for a woman, for a wife, what a woman should be. Maybe like his mother, who left him only because she wanted more for him.

I think that's what he wanted from me. Because I've always had this ambitious thing about me, I was hooked to that too. And soon I sensed that, well, with my intentions and my ambition and the way I had grown up, if he really wants *me,* then he's got to be ambitious himself. But anyone could see that in him. So I began looking over his head, too, thinking that there must be something he can see in me to make him feel this way about me. Because I know how I feel about myself. I know what I'm gonna try in life, I know this Trench Town thing is not gonna be my last days. Sometime, somehow, I'm gettin' out of *here.*

From then on, it seemed, Bob put his trust in me. I began answering his mother's letters to him, sending the information she needed to file his U.S. papers, and writing my own letters to her to tell her what was going on. We spent even more time together, and we usually talked a lot. And sometimes, when we rehearsed until late, and love was wakin', he'd say, "Why should you have to go?"

And I'd have to tell him, "But Aunty's waiting, and it's ten o'clock and you don't come in after *eight* for Aunty."

After eight she'd stay at the gate! Before eight you can stop at the gate and talk and kiss a little or so, but . . . ten o'clock, she's *there.* Standing her ground now, waiting! Oh Aunty! Her being like that would amuse Bob so! And if we had money, he had to take her something, like the Wincarnis wine she loved.

One night he was walking me home—it was within walking distance, so we'd always walk (slowly!) from Coxsone's to Trench Town—and he said to me, "Something is happening at the studio, it's happening every night." He explained that he'd usually go to bed when everything was over in the studio, when only the watchman was there, but that lately, as soon as he went to bed, a cat had started coming every night, making some weird sound, as if it were talking.

He looked pitiful. "And the cat cries, Rita," he said. "Like it's calling someone's name."

The next day, and every day after that, I'd ask what happened overnight, and he'd say, same thing. The cat came at a certain time every night and it was haunting him. It killed me to know that this was happening to him while I had a home to go to and my own room and a bed to sleep in. So one night I said, "Bob, I'm going to leave that window right over my bed open and tonight after you take me home you just walk through the window, come stay with me." And it wasn't about coming in to have sex, it was just to give him shelter.

But he said, "You sure? 'Cause Aunty miserable . . . ?"

And I said, "It doesn't matter, I can't bear to think of you with that cat. Let's try it."

That night he waited outside while I walked in the door. "Good night, Aunty, good night," I said.

"Why you come in so late?" she demanded. "It's nine and you remember you have the baby and you don't want to have no more baby because the baby father gone to England and . . ."

"Aunty, you know this isn't about babies," I said. "I'm trying to work at the studio, I'm trying my best, I promise . . ."

And she locked the door and I went to my room and as planned Bob came through the window. But just after he got inside she reappeared, bringing the baby to me, because she usually kept Sharon in her room until I got home. And there she is, with the baby in her arms, and Bob is creeping under the bed! And she looks . . . and—"Who is under there? I see something moving!"

I said no it wasn't . . . it must be Dream . . .

"No!" she shouted. "Dream is in his bed!" And she looked again and she said, "Jesus Christ, Rita, why you bring Robbie in here? You want to breed again? You want to have another baby? My Lord, no no, not in here . . . Let him come out—come out!"

I had never . . . I'd never felt . . . the blood from my body went . . . *tschoooooo* . . . all the way down to my toes!

Poor Bob. I wasn't even sorry for myself like I was sorry for him. And she kept insisting that he had to leave. I tried to explain, "Aunty, really now. I never intended for him to sleep with me, I was gonna make him sleep in Dream's room . . . but then I didn't want him to come in the door because you wouldn't allow him to. But he has nowhere to sleep, Aunty. He's sleeping on a door at the studio!"

But she said, "No no, next thing you come breeding here again and another baby . . . and this one that one . . . no no. Jesus! He has to go!"

So I said, "Well, if he has to go, I'm going with him." I was furious by that time. I said, "You know, Aunty, that's sin, to make him leave at this hour of night, for him to walk back up there alone, in the dark! Anything could happen to him, Aunty, they could kill him, thievery . . ."

"No no!" she insisted. "I don't care!"

So I said, "Okay, Robbie, come." And I grabbed his hand and went toward the door.

But she said, "No! He has to walk back through the window! Wherever he walk in, let him walk out!"

And so poor Bob had to go back out through that window. And I walked out the door, while Aunty was saying, "Must I lock the door?"

"Go ahead," I said. "Because I'm not coming back. I'm gonna stay with Robbie tonight. I'm not coming back."

"And who will look after the baby when the baby wakes up?"

I knew she was just trying to make me feel guilty, so that didn't bother me. I didn't care, I just walked, thinking, no, this is it now. I didn't want to be rude to her—this was the first time I'd ever slept out—but I was not going to let Bob sleep alone, in that place, again. I grabbed a blanket—*her* blanket, which was *my* blanket . . .

As we walked away, onto the dark road, Bob said, "Rita, you sure? Aunty gonna kill you tomorrow."

And I said what I really meant. "I don't care."

We were both so exhausted by the time we got back to the studio that we lay down on the door and fell right to sleep. Until there was the sound he'd been describing, *"baow."* I lay there, listening, aware that he was awake too.

"You see?" he whispered. "Every night it happens about one and it continues until five, six in the morning, just straight."

And I listened . . . and then the thing, whatever it was, came into the room—not physically, but the sensation. And I went . . . out, not unconscious, but I couldn't speak. I was trying to let Bob know how I was feeling, but the words wouldn't come although I knew I was awake. Then I felt hot and started to shake—and he said, "Lord have mercy!"—and ran out to get the watchman, yelling, "Come quick, something happening to Rita!" And they came in and threw water on me, and when I came to myself I realized that *something* had happened, though I couldn't tell what. And Bob said, "I told you, I told you, Rita, this is what's been happening."

Next morning I went home and had to beg Aunty. I said, "Now, Aunty, we have to look out for Robbie, at least I do. Aunty, please, we won't have sex or anything. But let him sleep for a time in the room with Dream. It's very important. Please."

It was now clear to everyone, even Aunty, that Bob and I were serious about each other. I had started really thinking about him, trying to decide whether this guy could be the man for me. I didn't want to make another mistake. Besides, Bob was a good example, a good role model as we'd say today. What I liked, to begin with, was that he approached me with a sense of consciousness about me as a whole person; I was very impressed by that. Here is one who really has a different direction, I thought. It wasn't all about "Hey, can I touch your tits" or "Let's have sex," the usual teenage lust. It was something a little bit more, maybe because he was a country boy. But he had reservations and respect about that aspect of life. After six or seven, fine, but during the day you could see he was about something else: Let's either make music or talk about the future.

I really felt that this boyfriend of mine was different from other guys I'd met, and that I might be able to learn something from him. That had to be good for me, I thought, and for Sharon too, because even though Aunty was in charge, once you have a baby you're a woman, whether you're twelve or twenty. I knew that in the long run Sharon was my responsibility, even though Bob was so adaptable to her. He really did love her, really saw her through the eyes of one who *wanted* to see. And even though I was making a little money at Coxsone's and was able to contribute at home, I couldn't contribute very much. Bob was aware of that, and he began to contribute things, too. He was always making sure that Sharon and I had what he thought was best for us.

When we started to date, he'd introduced me to his friend Georgie. Anything you want, Bob said, anything you need, just ask Georgie. If I'm not here, here is Georgie till I come. Georgie was an older man, like many of Bob's friends. Older or not, they were his pals, though, because Bob was inclined that way. I wouldn't say he was above his time or above his age, but his level was always more mature. He would often bring a bundle of okra or some callaloo or some oranges from his friend Vincent Ford (called Tata). It was in Tata's kitchen that Bob ended up living, which quieted Aunty for a while—but it should come as no surprise that in Tata's kitchen Bob and I first made love. His friend Bragga would bring me fresh cow's milk in the mornings, always with a cheerful "Everything aright?" And I would say, and oh, I really meant it, "Yeah, man, everything *cool.*"

I often think about men like Tata and Bragga and Georgie, who became my friends too, men whom I knew Bob would look out for, men who always looked out for Bob. Tata was credited as the cowriter of "No Woman No Cry," which Bob did to honor such a close friend, another father figure like Coxsone. Sometimes Tata would come up to see us and then walk home with Bob, and I'd feel better that there were the two of them, turning back into the dangerous streets of Trench Town in the dark hours of the night.

As for Georgie, who in that very song, "would make the fire light," he is still around and still my friend. I have vivid memories of times when Georgie did indeed make the fire light, and it was true that it would burn "through the night." Bob always wrote about real things, about his feelings. They would be playing guitar and all of us singing and drinking cornmeal porridge or sharing whatever was cooked for the day. All the rest of that song turned out to be true, too. And because Bob was so real, so true to himself, I feel that I need to insist on that here. Aunty always said, "Don't tell no stories," by which she meant lies. So this is not a "story," this is my life.

One holiday some of Coxsone's major artists—the Wailers and Soulettes, Delroy Wilson, the Paragons—were performing live at an all-day dance on Bournemouth Beach in Rockfort. It was a beautiful day, with puffy clouds in a blue sky—Jamaica's best weather—and the roar of the ocean and the bright sun seemed to calm everyone down. Before we went on Bob and I slipped away from the crowd, and found a secluded cove, and started to sing. By then he had his own guitar and always had it with him, and he was forever saying, "Let's try this, and this and that"— he would want to practice twenty-four hours a day! That day he said, "Let's just rehearse a little, because today we have to be good. There's a lot of young people here, and this is their exposure to the dancehall type of people, the wild guys and girls, and we have to show them the best of us."

This was the serious Bob, the moral Bob I admired. He made me *want* to try, by trusting my musical instincts and making me responsible for harmonies. But demanding perfection. And so we were there rehearsing in this little cove, and oh, we were suddenly so taken away, and looking into each other's eyes and singing, and then we put our mouths to each other's—we were still singing—as if we were giving oxygen to each other, giving each other mouth-to-mouth resuscitation! And I'm thinking, is this love? And the song with that title hadn't even been written yet! Is this love? And then we're kissing and laughing and looking into each other's eyes and I'm thinking, wow, this is *magic!* This is *magic,* I'm in *love* with this guy, I *love* him! We *love* each other!

We got married on impulse, because Bob's mother had sent for him. Unlike a lot of girls, I hadn't been dreaming of being married at that age, it wasn't something I had in mind. I never thought about "my wedding day." To begin with, we didn't have anything to be married on, and in those days in Jamaica, you couldn't wake up one day and want to marry, you had to plan, and you had to save money for it.

But Cedella Malcolm Marley had married Edward Booker, an American. Having gotten her own legal papers, she could now sponsor her son. So Bob had to emigrate, but he said he wouldn't leave unless I eventually went with him. Though we were well in love, we hadn't even talked about getting married until this happened. Bob thought that if we weren't married before he left, I would find another boyfriend. I don't know if that would have happened—maybe—but he wouldn't allow it to happen. And by then he was my "straight boyfriend," as we say in Jamaica. I was neither seeing nor thinking about another man. He was my Number One. Plus he was now getting some recognition; he was waiting for his muse, his music was playing on the radio. We both thought we were made for each other.

Our plan was that he was going to sponsor me when he got to

Delaware. Even after his mother's experience, we refused to believe that this couldn't happen quickly and easily. We had no idea that things would turn out the way they did. But I think I got involved with the Robbie I knew because he was so clearly a strong young man. He was very straight-forward and strong-headed, in terms of "This is what I want to do, this is what I'm going to do." And very serious about his family and life. His spirit was there, too, the strength of his spirit showed. I guess I have a strong spirit too, to identify one. As partners and soul mates there was some chemistry that was natural and positive. And our astrological signs were right—him being an Aquarian and me a Leo, we faced each other on the zodiac. And I think our relationship came out of wanting, needing, see-ing the need in each other. My need is in you, I need someone like you. To help me, to make me what I am, what I want to be. And I think we did great.

We were married, at eleven in the morning on February 10, 1966, a couple of days after his twenty-first birthday. Bob got ready at Aunty's and I went to my Uncle Cleveland's, where my cousin Yvonne got me really sharp. Then we met at the office of the Justice of the Peace. Bob had on a black suit and fancy shoes that Coxsone had bought for him; I wore a bor-rowed mother-of-pearl tiara, and a ruffled white wedding dress cut just below the knee, with a short lace veil (both made by Aunty, of course, who—without my knowledge—had gone with Bob to buy the ring with his small savings). I was nineteen going on twenty, very happy, but almost unable to believe I was actually getting married.

Sharon was not quite a year. Aunty had put her in a chair, where she had been sleeping but then woke up just in time to take the wedding pic-ture. She stood up in the chair, very surprised at all the excitement, and just as the photographer was clicking the shutter she pulled up her little dress, and she peed! In the photograph her dress is lifted up, and she's standing with the pee coming down and looking at it!

We had a wonderful day. Aunty cooked curried goat and rice with green bananas, and made what we call a "three-sister" cake. Our pictures show how much in love we were. We look as if we're thinking, how did this happen? But it's happening! We're husband and wife! But oh, we were so . . . like twins.

The Wailing Wailers had a concert at National Stadium that night, on the bill with the Jackson Five. Sometime during the show, we heard on the mike, "Congratulations to Bob and Rita, who got married today!" We were absolutely surprised—Bob said, "Who told them!"—and the Wailers gave a first-class performance. That night we were so happy we went home and made love all night.

Two days later, he left for Delaware. This was dread. After taking him to the airport, I came home crying, feeling empty and lonely, and shocked, as if I'd been caught in a whirlwind and set down somewhere strange. I remember going to the studio with Bunny and Peter and Dream, recording a song called "I've Been Lonely So Long, Don't Seem Like Happiness Will Come Along." Five days later I got my first letter. "My Dear Wife," it said. "How are you? I miss you very much, it's very cold here in America."

chapter three
CHANCES ARE

DURING THE TIME I was getting to know Bob, he'd been exposing me
to the faith of Rastafari, which began in the early twentieth century
with Marcus Garvey, a Jamaican who was also from St. Ann. Garvey went
to New York, where he founded the Universal Negro Improvement Association, to encourage black pride and advocate the repatriation of black people to Africa.

Some Jamaicans paid particular attention to Garvey's prophecy that an
African king would deliver us from our situation as colonized people, and
they came to believe the Ethiopian ruler Emperor Haile Selassie I to have
been that person. Selassie's original name was Ras Tafari; his followers and
believers are Rastafarians, Rastas for short.

Before the sixties, no one outside Jamaica knew much about Rastas.
Within Jamaica, ordinary citizens viewed them as "blackheart" men who
lived in the gully and were always smoking ganja (an East Indian word for
marijuana). People said they would steal your children away. They didn't cut
their hair or straighten it, instead letting it grow naturally into "locks," or

"dreadlocks." The word "dread," now used in many ways, has its origins in the Rastafari challenge to Jamaican colonial authority. Which of us is "dreadful"?

In Jamaica, Rasta was the *last* thing you wanted your children to be involved with. People said it turned its followers worthless, that besides smoking ganja Rastas didn't eat properly, wash their hair, or brush their teeth. Only the worst things were said about them—no one mentioned the Rasta message of peace and love and understanding and justice, its refusal of pain and abuse, although they silently agreed with its message of black pride.

For black people everywhere, the 1960s was a time of consciousness-raising. In the United States, people were considering not only "Black Is Beautiful" but "Black Power." These ideas reached us too; at one time we were all carving small black fists from wood and selling them at the record shop. People bought them to wear around their necks. For one album cover the Wailers posed for photographs holding toy guns and wearing the berets usually associated with the Black Panthers.

As soon as Aunty allowed Bob to take me out, he'd begun to show me the Rasta way to live. "You're a queen, a black queen," he said. "You're pretty just as you are, you don't need to do anything else. You don't have to straighten your hair, you can wear it natural." After so many years of submitting weekly to a hot comb, I put mine away. Bob was also very intent on telling me how great black people were, and how far we'd come because of Marcus Garvey. Aunty was big on Garvey too, and had even given me a book about him, so I already knew about repatriation and the story of the Black Star Line, and was somewhat conscious to begin with. And certainly very aware, from an early age, of the condescension behind being called "blackie tootus."

But after I stopped pressing my hair Aunty began to worry, my God, is Rita smoking that stuff, that terrible stuff that would make you go crazy and put you to prison! And of course she wanted to blame Bob, because I *had* started smoking a little herb, though I thought I was doing a good job of hiding it from her. When I smoked in my room, I'd squirt baby powder into the air to cover the smell. But I liked smoking for the way it made me feel—cooled out and meditative—and I think if I were to blame anyone it would have to be my father. (Though I don't blame anyone and have no regrets.) Papa was nowhere near Jamaica when I started smoking, but I remembered that sometimes he'd had a smell about him that I liked. It was only after he'd gone out to smoke that he smelled like that—which would piss Aunty off, until she'd threaten him: "Don't even come near this house!" So when I discovered that I'm liking it, I'm saying *tschoo!* It's from my father, it really doesn't have anything to do with Bob. It isn't Bob!

While we were courting, one of the many things he and I had often talked about was what you should and shouldn't eat. At the time, like most people who lived in Trench Town, I ate pork. It was always available to poor people and made up a large part of our diet—we ate trotters, pig feet, and the pig's tail that we put in our peas and rice. Stew peas and rice was one of our favorite dishes. When Bob mentioned that the Rastafari believed that you were not supposed to eat the pig, I thought he was crazy. I said, "What are you talking about? The sweetest meat, and that's what I was grown on?"

But I listened to his explanation from the Old Testament and considered that maybe there was some truth to it. Still, how could I not eat something when I had no money to make my own choices? Without money, I had to eat what Aunty gave me, and I'd wanted to avoid her discovery that I was changing my diet. This was part of her old fear, that the Trench Town rude boys would get to me. But the fight was unavoidable. Bob was now passing through the house to get me for studio. One day she'd been cooking callaloo and codfish, which traditionally is cooked down with pork. I went into the kitchen and, as calmly as I could, said, "Aunty, I won't be eating any of that callaloo today because of the pork."

And she went crazy! She told everybody—calling over the fence to our neighbor Mother Rose, "You know Rita just tell me she not eating any of the dinner because pork in there!" And Mother Rose said, "I told you that boy . . ." And they started to put the blame on "Robbie and this Rasta thing." But I was stubborn, and refused to listen, and from then on Aunty realized that I was going through changes and was trying to become more conscious, and she accepted the fact that I had to find out certain things for myself. Such as, what was really black? And why is black so *black*? Why is black so black and white so *white*?

The interesting thing to me now is that everyone wanted to blame all my decisions on other people, as if I couldn't possibly be thinking on my own. But I began to feel that we were the generation who had come to rise up. Also, Bob had introduced me to some of the Rasta elders, and after meeting them a few times and listening to what they had to say, I was convinced that these people were for real. The whole thing seemed intelligent to me; it wasn't just about smoking herb, it was more a philosophy that carried a history with it. That's what really pulled my interest, the powerful history that hadn't been taught to me in school.

I was going through those changes but I wasn't, as everyone believed, going crazy. I thought I was opening up to more wisdom and felt I should share it. I had a strong religious impulse to begin with—as a child in church, I used to get the spirit, jumping and shouting, speaking in tongues and going into trances. Long before I met Bob, I'd been reading my Bible. Now I turned to preaching the faith of Rastafari—wherever I went I'd talk about black pride and raising ourselves up. Whenever I took a bus, I'd go to the front after I boarded and say, "Good morning, brothers and sisters!" My friends said, "Rita, you sure you're okay?" And I would say, "Fine, fine . . ." Then I started to wear my nurse's uniform, and tied a rope of red, gold, and green (the Rasta colors) around my waist, and people began to whisper, "You know she's crazy, she's getting crazy, what a shame after all the money her aunty spent on her." And Aunty's friends were telling her, "See now? The girl is crazy—get her father here."

But in the morning or the afternoon some people would *wait* for my bus. They'd say, "Any bus Rasta woman take"—Rasta Queen, they called me—"any bus 'Queenie' on, we go on Queenie bus." Everybody knew that when Queenie was on the bus, it was going to be Bible time. "Queenie gonna teach today," they'd say. Sometimes I would have my rod, like a walking stick. I thought I was on a mission and didn't feel in any way strange about it. I wouldn't wear bangles or earrings or perfume, only ordinary sandals, nothing sleeveless, my dress had to cover my ankles, my hair had to be covered, I used to keep it so tied up . . .

I realize now that whatever you put yourself through to be where you are today is all a part of you. I wasn't crazy, I was simply trying to find out who I was, and where, and why. Nevertheless, without my knowledge, Aunty wrote my father: "You better come get Rita out of here, she's mix up with these guys and this Rasta thing."

Though Papa always kept in touch, it wasn't until I saw his response to Aunty's letter that I knew she'd written him. In Trench Town back then when you got a letter from anywhere overseas, everyone knew about it: "*Ooh*—you get a letter from America, let me see the envelope!" Or: "Miz Britton get a letter today from America, I saw it in the post, man! Is only you get a letter wid dose red stamp wid de president on it . . . !"

Although it was addressed to Aunty, I opened the letter and read: "Dear Sister Vie, I am very surprised to hear about Rita. But don't abuse her. Is she keeping herself clean? That is most important to me. If she's clean she'll be fine, because she's very intelligent. Don't fret yourself or worry her."

When I confronted Aunty, she said simply, "I had to." But by then she had divorced Mr. Britton, and I had become another breadwinner for our family, helping to support us through my work in the studio and with the Soulettes. Papa was still living in London, playing his sax and doing whatever he had to do to survive. He had been joined by Alma Jones, a Jamaican woman with whom he was to have a long relationship, and who later on would be very kind to me at a time when I very much needed some kindness. Their union had produced my sister Margaret and brother George. The last thing Papa needed at that moment was a sullen nineteen-year-old on his hands. Aunty took stock of the situation and said no more about sending me away.

Wesley, who had always lived with us, had grown into a young man now, and after Bob left for Delaware he had joined the police force. In Jamaica, police are rotated among parishes, so he used to spend most of his time living in police lodgings and came home only on holidays or weekends. He would arrive in his uniform, the talk of the town because, *ooh,* Uncle Wesley is a policeman! (This was a big thing to be in the early sixties.) As with me, people made a fuss over his bright, even teeth. Always smiling, very charming and mannerly, he was known locally as Mr. Tooths—definitely "Mister," because he had become the man of the house after Aunty's divorce. And took his role seriously, as I would find out.

A month after Bob left we learned that Jamaica was to receive a visit from Haile Selassie. By the time his plane touched down, on April 21, 1966, a huge crowd—more than a hundred thousand people—had gathered. Most of them were Rastas or members of other African-centered Jamaican groups. Because of the masses of people, I never got any farther than the road to the airport, so I stopped and waited for the motorcade to pass by. Bob hadn't wanted me to go, but I said I was going anyway. Everybody was on the street smoking and having a nice time—it felt like freedom, freedom for black people, to see this black supremacy coming in real life.

I kept looking into the different cars and finally I saw him, this little man in an army uniform with a military-looking hat. Rastas believe that when you see your black king you will see your black god, and so when he was almost close up to me I said to myself, is that the man they say is God? They must be crazy. I didn't believe, looking at him, I just didn't believe.

Short little man in his army uniform. Quite simple. With one hand he was waving side to side, and I thought, oh please God, could this be what I read about? Show me if what they say about this man is true, show me a sign so I can see, so I can put my faith *some*where, I need to hold on to *some*thing.

And just as I thought my prayer wasn't working, Haile Selassie turned in my direction and waved. There was something about the middle of his palm that struck me—I saw a black print. And I said, oh my God, the Bible says that when you see him you will know him by the nail prints in his hand. Most people think I'm lying, but I'm not lying, it happened. I don't know if it's mind over matter, but I was looking for something to identify with. And there it was.

I yelled, "Oh my God," and went home screaming and cheering. And Aunty said, "Lord have mercy, there she goes! Now she's truly mad!" It had been raining and I was soaked, but I didn't care. Aunty thought I was completely out of it, but for me it was an awakening. For the emperor to be waving at me!

As soon as I got to my room I started a letter: "Dear Robbie, I just came back from seeing His Majesty, and I swear I have seen him . . ." I gave Bob the whole picture of the crowd and people beating drums in the street and smoking herb and the police didn't lock up anybody! What a day to remember in Jamaica! As for what I saw—ain't nobody gonna take that from me!

But Bob's response was, "Dear Rita, I got your letter, please take it easy, don't go anywhere. Don't go smoking at anybody's place, stay at home and read and take care of yourself and the baby!"

The first days after Bob went to Delaware, I'd been devastated. Totally devastated, really lost. What is this? I kept asking myself. Married two days ago, madly in love, and now he's gone? In my head—and sometimes aloud—I kept singing all the love songs I knew, but they kept turning into songs about loneliness, and how much I missed him. But at the same time I had to remind myself that I was now a married woman, for one thing, and two, I had to remember that my husband had gone to find a job and I had a daughter who had to be maintained. All of this brought me back to the same position I'd been in before the whole idea of marriage had intervened: Should I carry on singing or go back to nursing? At night I'd lie awake, trying to decide. Should I go find me a job, or what? Should I continue to be around Peter and Bunny and all the others at Studio One? Dream—or Vision, as he was now known—was ready and always available, and as the Soulettes still had a name we figured we still had a chance. If I wanted to, of course. We had maintained our connection to the studio and Coxsone continued to ask us to do background vocals for other groups—Delroy Wilson, Lord Creator, Tony Gregory are a few I remember.

Bob didn't want me to go to the studio, it seemed. "Stay home and take care of your baby," he would write, always "stay home." He would never say "Go find you a job," though he knew I had to have money coming in from somewhere. We wrote each other almost every day. Letters would be in and out, and if that postman passed my gate without stopping, my heart sank, because I'd look for a letter every day, no matter if I'd gotten one yesterday or the day before. But despite Bob's constant advice to stay home and take care of Sharon, Dream and I went to Studio One whenever we were asked, to do background vocals for Peter or for Bunny or whoever else Coxsone was recording and wanted us to work with.

Nevertheless, even with keeping myself busy and Bob's letters keeping up my spirits, sometimes I'd feel lonely and lost after a studio session, just thinking, when will I see my husband? And missing him—everything about him, his voice, his music—and then going home and saying to myself, when am I going to go to America? I wasn't thinking about him coming home, it was all about my going to America. That separation was a trial for me. I was a strong young lady, true, but it would get me down sometimes when people said, "I heard you're married to Robbie, where is he?" One of his old girlfriends, a girl named Cherry, even accosted me to say, "That was my man!" I went through all that without him even being around to defend me. But Bunny told her not to mess with me, that Bob would come home and kill her if she did!

It took Bob a while to reveal to his mother that he was married. Cedella Booker had known about me, or at least about a girl named Rita, from my letters. She knew we had been dating, knew I was his girlfriend, but nothing about the wedding. After he finally admitted to it, and she asked him to describe me, he'd said, "Oh Mommy, if you should see her you'd like her, she walks and she rolls." And Mrs. Booker said, "What do you mean by that?" And he said, "If she walking and you see her from the back, she rolls!" When I heard this story I wondered what could he mean? Until I realized it was my knock knees that did that! (Some people think it's sexy.)

Married or not, his mother sent her sister to check out my house—I guess to find out where I lived, whether I was good- or bad-looking, whatever—I never knew what they were looking for. But when her sister came to see where I'd been raised and saw that the walls of my room were decorated with pictures from magazines—like all teenagers I had put up posters and pinup pictures—Mrs. Booker's sister wrote her to say that I was such a poor girl that I lived in a house with cardboard walls! Plus, I had a baby! So in America they were all disappointed. But by then there was nothing to be done; we were on our way.

It wasn't long—only eight months—before Bob decided to leave Delaware. His mother said he'd been worried about me; she was surprised that he loved me more than he loved the United States. She couldn't understand why, even though she'd never met me. She had been sure that America was his dream, and his family there had done everything to entice him to stay—even brought him pretty girls *after* they found out he was married.

But Bob had his own reasons for leaving America. Poor thing. He'd worked first in a Chrysler factory, then at the Hotel Dupont in Wilmington. When at last he gave up he wrote me, "I'm coming home, I'm sick of this place. Today, while I was vacuuming, the vacuum bag burst and all that dust went up in my face."

The poor boy!

"If I stay here, this is gonna kill me," he wrote. "It will give me all kinds of sickness! I'm a singer, I'm not this, I'm coming home."

The whole homecoming scene was *so* very good—and felt so long over-due! It didn't seem like eight months; it seemed like forever that I had waited for that moment, to see him coming out, into the terminal. And there he was looking at me, his head to the side as if he was just longing to put eyes on me, just the same way I was feeling. And poor Bob, you looked at him and you just felt sorry for him! And I keep feeling this way about him, even now. My love for him is a deep, true, lasting love, of course—but there was something about sorrying for him that still is in me. Though he had left with only one bag, now he had one over his shoulder and another, a suitcase, in his hand. We hugged and kissed, and he said, "Yeah, man, I'm back, my mother sent some things for you and Sharon and I bring a dress for you and things like that." I just had a chance to say *"Ooooh"* before Dream and Aunty grabbed him. And Sharon even remembered how to say "Bahu!" We were all so glad to see him!

But then, on the way home, he said to me, "Why you no fix up yourself, what happened to your hair?" (I was wearing it natural.) He seemed puz-zled more than critical, and I guess, after American women, I looked dif-ferent. With him gone, I'd been into reading and trying to confirm that whatever he had said wasn't simply herb talk, or something he had picked up on the street. And ever since seeing the dark spot on Haile Selassie's hand, I'd felt more secure about being a part of the Rastafarian movement.

But the day he came home none of that stayed on my mind very long. We got home, ate dinner, played a little music, sneaked out to the alley for a little smoke, and then went straight to bed—and it was like *whooo*—heaven! If that's how heaven is, fine, I want to go there!!

And even after the first excitement wore off, I noticed a little extra affection being laid on me, whether from missing me or any other reason, I didn't know. Whatever, I was very happy about it. Love can bring out the best in anyone, I guess. And it was great to realize all over again how much we loved each other. This is where we had a nice time. Yes, definitely, this is about a nice time.

The little money Bob brought back was just enough to go into the studio with Bunny and Peter to record a few of his earliest songs, like "Nice Time": "Long time we no have a nice time/ Long time I don't see you/ this is my heart to rock you steady . . ." As he did then, and as he always would, he was just naturally singing about his feelings. So we went into lovemaking and family making. First was to be Cedella, my second daughter, named after Bob's mother, but whose pet name is "Nice Time," just like the song.

As soon as Bob came home, I had to get to work. Music is art, but it's also business, and all three of the Wailers were more into writing songs and rehearsing. To keep the rights to their music, we had begun our own company, Wail'NSoul'M (for the Wailers and the Soulettes). At one point we were actually producing, manufacturing our own records. I was still singing (Bob and I recorded a cover version around this time, along with Peter, Bunny, Cecile, and Hortense, of "Hold On to This Feeling"). But someone had to be going out to make sure the record shops and the radio stations had the records. You had to be on the streets to service them every day.

We were still living at Aunty's house on Greenwich Park Road, where she had added on a room for us. Our bedroom faced the road, so in the daytime Bob and I curtained off part of it and made the front into a little shop, where we sold our 45rpm "dub plates"—in those days everything was on these seven-inch vinyl recordings. Some days we'd sell three, some days six, sometimes as many as twenty-five, out of a cashier's booth, a little cage we'd constructed. I never imagined that cage as part of history, but there are two replicas of it now, one at the Bob Marley Museum in Kingston and the other at Universal Studios in Orlando, Florida.

I also made deliveries on my bike. Aunty was a bicycle rider, so she had trained me to do the same—"Take the bicycle, run go buy a needle." It was because of the bike and the shop that I found a woman friend for life, Minion Smith (later Phillips). When we met I was still searching, looking for more strength to confirm my feelings of faith in Rastafari, and I saw Minion as a sister who was already involved in the struggle in Jamaica, where white supremacy and class barriers were so defined. Her mother's Jewish family had fled the Holocaust and her father was Jamaican, and they lived uptown, in middle-class Kingston. Minion—called Minnie—was one of the first young women from that area to show an interest in Rasta and, as expected, her family thoroughly disapproved. Tall and beautiful and very militant, she used to come down to our shop to buy records, and I liked her style, her sandy brown dreads, the way she carried herself. Seeing her in Trench Town, I thought, wow, there goes a Rasta sister who looks confident and *strong*.

That strength was so appealing. During those early sixties years, being young and female and endorsing Rastafari was a sure way to become an outcast, and seen as crazy and strange, even more so than the men. But like them, Minnie—the only other young Rasta woman I'd met so far—and I were simply searching for a way out of the discrimination and rejection we felt all around us, and trying to understand that we were not from the nowhere in which we felt stranded, but had a heritage in Africa, that we had roots.

Sometimes I'd get on my bicycle and meet Sister Minnie part way, between Trench Town and where she lived, and we'd talk about Black Power and Malcolm X and Angela Davis and Miriam Makeba. To make extra money I was making dashikis, and she'd take them uptown with the bead jewelry she made and sell them at the university. Over the years she has given me a lot of strength and support, but we had a link at the first. Sometimes you meet somebody and you know right away, wow, we're going to be friends for a long time.

Late one afternoon, riding home from a record shop in Half Way Tree, which is more than three miles from Trench Town, I was hit by a car and thrown from the bicycle. In my carrier on the back I had a load of records, to be delivered from orders we'd gotten for Wail'NSoul'M Recordings. I was more embarrassed than frightened, because I was accustomed to this daily three-mile ride from Trench Town to Crossroads, and from Crossroads to Halfway Tree. Sometimes I'd go back to downtown Kingston, too, where all the famous record shops were, like Randy's and KG's. Everybody knew me, everybody looked out for me: "Oh Rasta Queenie come! What records you have for us today?" I was a favorite because we were carrying new stuff that was in demand, a little of the Wailers, a little of the Soulettes, so it was very exciting. And I was so young and full of enthusiasm, carefree and happy despite being poor, and loving every moment of my life and thinking, one day we're gonna be somebody, or one day we'll have money, or one day, we're gonna have enough to eat!

Eating—specifically, what am I gonna cook for our dinner tonight?— was exactly what I'd been thinking about when the car knocked me over. It had never occurred to me that I might stop concentrating on the road, and when it happened I was totally surprised and frightened. Why had this happened to me? By then people on the street were used to seeing me, so all around me I heard "Queenie, your records!" and "Queenie, you all right?" Everyone tried to help me, people gathered in the street. "Queenie, man, you no fear ride the bicycle?" "Queenie, man, you forget you aren't a car?" And I'm thinking, yeah, that's true! I'm gonna stop doing this, I'm gonna give this over to one of the guys! I'd hurt myself, too, but I was just glad the accident hadn't been fatal, and when Bob saw me, and saw what the bicycle looked like, that was the day I stopped riding to sell records!

I'd been worried about cooking because most of Bob's friends had started coming to our house, and they had to be fed, that's how they were. Aunty's place had become a social scene. They'd stay all day and they would make music, smoke a little (well away from the house), talk, make more music, tell jokes, make more music, play a little football (soccer). A lot of people learned from Bob the discipline and patience required for making music. As Ansel Cridland of the Meditations was to say years later, "Is not like a thing that is just run in there and look at the clock and trying to get it done in . . . an hour or something. It's a time. And when you spend time on your work you get better results. Working with Bob Marley was a great experience."

Still, I was the one who had to think about practical things, like making sure we had something to eat, and paying for the electricity we used playing records over and over, because even though we weren't paying Aunty rent, it was only right that we paid for the power. So if I wasn't thinking about the next meal, or the electric bill, I was worrying about how we'd pay the bill for the bed and dresser we'd bought on credit at Courts Furniture Store in Crossroads.

Sometimes Aunty would say she didn't see any life in this; she'd be upset because it didn't look like there was going to be a better day. I was always under that microscope of hers, and she would make sure I knew it. But then our music began to be played on the radio and the sound systems; the street people were reacting to our music, and after that we started doing a little TV. Aunty liked that, she liked the charisma, she liked the excitement. And now, when people would ask her, "How is Rita?" she'd say with a smile, "Oh she's not too bad. She turned out—not as we wanted, but you know, t'ank God, she's not too bad!"

My brother Wesley, though, was furious when he found out about my Rastafari beliefs. Though Bob and I were already married, as a policeman

Wesley felt he had a little authority, and he had an attitude, you might say. "Do you think it is right," he asked me when he came home from one of his parish assignments, "after all the money Aunty and I spent on you, that you end up like this? What are you getting out of it? You think because you're married you're big? You're still under our protection, and you have no right to be a Rasta! That's being worthless!"

I said to him, "You have no right to be a policeman, you're a Babylon!"

And he boxed me! Slapped my face—*pow*! I cried and thought, I'm still being treated like a child. What the hell is this, where's my life? But I was determined, despite all these objections.

When Bob heard about my brother having hit me, he cried too—even more than I had. He felt humiliated that this had happened to his wife, and there was nothing he could do because we were living in *their* house. He felt he was no longer just "Robbie"—Aunty still called him "the boy"—but a married man with responsibilities. So he said, "You know what we should do? Come, let's go to *my* home."

He meant his birthplace in the countryside at Nine Miles, St. Ann. The idea appealed to me, since I'd never been there and it could be something new. But despite being married and nearly twenty-two years old, I was still so young and inexperienced that I said, "Oh, first I have to ask Aunty!"

But I also didn't feel Bob was capable or prepared enough to take up responsibility for me, wholly and solely, 100 percent.

Nevertheless, we decided to go. I was already pregnant with Cedella, and Aunty said, "You're crazy, you're gonna go down there and tu'n wu'th-less, you're gonna be a country woman, what is he gonna give you? You're gonna do farming? You're gonna plant yams and cabbage?"

And Bob's mother wrote that St. Ann would be the end of us, that he should come back to Delaware and be a gentleman—the type who wears neckties and works nine to five and commutes was what she wanted. You're going back to the careless life, she said, the life that doesn't show money-making. You and Rita have no ambition!

Like many other parents the world over, Jamaican parents wanted you to make money, but only the way they'd intended. Otherwise they were upset with you. How dare you be what you want to be! But Bob had his directions and I believed they were right for him and so I encouraged him to follow them. I felt I would always be by his side. Later on I was given a lot of scorn, and many accusations came my way for urging him to remain conscious of his calling and his religion and his power. But then I said, "If going to St. Ann is what he wants, I'm gonna do it. Whatever my husband wants me to do."

chapter four
TO LOVE SOMEBODY

Even before we decided to go to St. Ann, we'd been talking about the changes in Aunty, who had started to act a little suspicious—or maybe just condescending—in response to everything we did. Bob felt that she was getting a bit of a sore eye with us being around so long and not able to get out of her place. I think what offended her most was our refusal to eat from her pot, because she cooked pork whenever she felt like, which of course was her right. I understood that, and usually cooked our food separately, but I guess it didn't make any difference. Bob and I had discussed the situation for many, many nights, as he was getting very unhappy and had begun to spend most of his time across the street, rather than staying in Aunty's yard and hearing himself constantly referred to as "the boy" or included with his friends as "dem boys."

Our plan was to go to Nine Miles and live in the house his father had given his mother, which was then standing empty. If we spent some time there and saved a little money, we figured, maybe we would be able to afford rent so that we could eventually come out of Aunty's place. Or maybe we could build a house in Nine Miles, though the fact that I was all for going there didn't entirely put Bob's mind at ease. "There's no water, no electricity, it's not like you're used to," he kept saying. And I kept answering, "Well, let's just try it. I want to. I want to go there, see what it's like." I felt it was compulsory for me to have this experience, because I didn't know his family and wanted to know where he was coming from. All I knew about St. Ann was that Marcus Garvey had come from there, too.

I know my enthusiasm made Bob happy anyway, and I guess we were so in love we didn't care where we were as long as we were together. This was when he recorded "Chances Are"—which, as usual, was about the life we were leading: "Chances are we're gonna leave now/ chances are hang on right now/ though our days are filled with sorrows/ I see years of bright tomorrows . . ." I kept my eyes on those "bright tomorrows."

I was so excited, so eager to go when the time came, that even Aunty's continual grumbling didn't bother me. I was like a child! I went shopping because we had to carry flour and rice and sugar, since Bob said there weren't any places to buy staple foods there. I packed the suitcase he'd brought from America, all the while listening to Aunty in the background: "Where you think you're going, you don't know, you don't know, you never did this before, they might take advantage of you . . . You might get sick, what can they give you if you get sick, what kind of clinic you're going to, to have your pregnancy tests?" And all of this and that.

Finally I said, "Don't worry so, Aunty! I'll write you, and I'll come back in about a week to let you know how we are, and if it don't suit, I'll come back altogether." And that seemed to satisfy her a little. In any case, she knew I'd keep my word about returning, because we were leaving Sharon with her while we settled ourselves, and Aunty knew we didn't plan to stay away from Sharon for too long.

At last it was time to go and we went down to Parade Square, in downtown Kingston, where the buses leave from, to catch a country bus, one of the painted buses that Jamaica is famous for, with names like "Amazing

Grace" or "Praise the Lord." Right away I said, "I want the window, I want the window!" But up to the last minute Bob was still questioning me. I'd already sat down and had my nose pressed to the glass when he said, "You sure?" Of course I was sure—to me it was like going on a long trip, plus the chance to learn more about him and how he grew up. And that to me would only mean I could love him even more.

It's about a seventy-five-mile journey to St. Ann, a couple of hours if you go in a car without making too many stops, but for more than four hours that country bus went slowly over winding mountain roads, stopping at every corner. And that was an experience! People got on with children, chickens, baskets full of every conceivable variety of fruit and vegetable. It didn't do too much for the morning sickness I was having—in fact, at one stop I had to jump off the bus to throw up—but I just kept looking out the window and trying to breathe the fresh air and stay positive.

When we finally got off after reaching Nine Miles, it seemed as if the whole neighborhood had come out to welcome us. It was a party! People were shouting, "Oh, it's Nesta!" and "Mas Nes come home!" and "Mas Nes come and bring him wife!" And then Bob pointed up this long hill, almost like a mountain, and said, "There's the house." And I looked up and said, "*That's* the house?" Because it wasn't what I thought of as a house, or at least not what we meant by a house in Trench Town. But he said, "Yes, that's it, let's go."

We climbed the hill, though it was getting dark and as he had warned, there was no electricity, so there were cries of "Where's the lamp? Where's the lamp?" And when we got inside and I saw there was no kitchen or toilet, I thought, oh my God, what did I get myself into. The smell of the place nauseated me, and I realized that this is what Aunty had been trying to warn me about. Still, I knew that going back to Trench Town right then was not an option. Whatever it is, I thought, that's what my husband has, and that's what I have to accept. I felt as if I had entered a different world.

Yet being surrounded by all these loving people who were so glad to see us felt just fine. His mother's sister's children, his cousins Clove, Dotty, and Helen, and his Aunt Amy and Aunty Ceta made me so welcome and kept saying, "Oh Mas Nes, what a nice girl you have for your wife!" "Anything you want, just call." It was decided that Clove was to be the helper for us, and to this day Clove is still Cedella's favorite, because it was she who nurtured me through my pregnancy.

That night I told Bob that it looked like life was going to be rough, but that I was ready. The next day we got started, trying to figure out how we were going to make things work. We had to rig up a bed from some boards and logs, and prepare a kitchen. But everybody came and gave a hand. And I really began to enjoy the adventure.

At the end of a week, as I'd promised, I took the bus back to Kingston to spend some time with Sharon and tell Aunty how fine we were, and so she could see for herself that I was still looking good. Naturally she was not impressed. "You better come back home!" was all she had to say. So I had to close my ears. I bought some things we needed, borrowed some curtains and sheets from Aunty, kissed Sharon and promised to take her with me next time, and went downtown and got back on the bus. I remember that this one was called "Promised Land."

And we began to live happily in that land—without worrying that Aunty was listening to everything we did and said. We could scream and be happy and be free! And that was such fun, to be totally independent. I felt, at last, like a grown woman. I'd get up in the morning and go to my *own* little kitchen, and bring water up the hill to *my* yard. Just the thought that we owned a *yard* now made Bob so proud. I think it added to his manhood. You could see the change in him, now that he was in his territory. And I could tell he was happy, because the first thing he took up after we unpacked was his little acoustic guitar. And right away he started to play and write songs—one of them mentions "the house on top of the hill."

And we did, indeed "do farming," as Aunty had predicted, on property that had belonged to his grandfather that someone in Bob's family allowed him to use. We planted yams, potatoes, and cabbage, and to get to our farm we had a pet donkey called Nimble. Every morning our friend Nimble would take me to the farm on his back, *clippety-clop, clippety-clop*, slowly, slowly, with Bob walking beside, and everybody would say, "Mas Nes!" "Hi, Mas Nes!" "Morning!" "Mornin', Miz Marley!" I felt like a queen on the back of that donkey! *Clippety-clop, clippety clop . . .* Country people don't just pass you, everybody we met said, "Howdy" or "How do you do?" And of course you had to reply: "Fine, thank you, ma'am!" or "God bless you, man." Bob once spoke about that in an interview: He said he never minded what people said about him, because where he came from in St. Ann people always blessed him, would say, "Good morning, Mas Nesta, God bless you, sir."

He treated Nimble like a son—even gave him vitamins! Wherever we went, Nimble was with us. I could hardly wait for the next morning to get on that donkey, with my big belly sticking out, to ride to the farm or to the village. Aunty had worried that I'd be pregnant without any attention; in the country, she was sure, there were no clinics. But Clove found one where I could be examined.

Every other week or so I went to Kingston to keep our business in perspective, to make sure we weren't losing money and customers, because that's what we ate our food from, the few records that sold. The bus would pass by our house early in the morning, around six-thirty, and I'd ride for three or four hours with the country people and their chickens and boxes from St. Ann to Kingston. I bought food in Kingston and took it back to the country to supplement what we managed to get there. And I'd better not forget to buy the tonic for Nimble—Bob would be so disappointed if I came back without Nimble's bee pollen! But whenever we were broke, or when my sugar or something else I couldn't afford was finished, or when I needed a pillowcase, I'd say, "Aunty, I need," and she'd say, "You have towels?" But I'd have to pay a price: One day I let her cut my dreadlocks off, because I knew she wanted to see me as she saw me, as the Rita, not the Rasta!

But I knew my locks would grow again, and more important, I knew where I wanted to be. The bus back to St. Ann left at five in the evening, and if you missed it you had to stay in Kingston overnight, there was no way you could get back except to hire a taxi, which I couldn't afford. So I always tried to be first on line at Parade when that bus opened its doors. Sometimes I'd take Sharon with me, to spend some time, because she hadn't yet started school. While I was gone Bob would clean the house and cook a meal so we'd have something to eat when we arrived. And there he'd be when the bus pulled up, just as he always said: "Rita, you look out for me when the bus come, I'll be standing up waiting for you." Years later, when he was called "the first Third World Superstar" and the "Negus" of reggae (meaning "the semidivine Ultimate"), I always wanted to remind people what led there. In St. Ann he had one pair of underpants, which I washed out every night. And if he cared enough to have a meal waiting for me when I came back from Kingston, I wanted to be back in time to care for him.

All in all I stayed healthy throughout my pregnancy, building Cedella in that country atmosphere; maybe that's why she's so strong today. And I was very active between going back and forth from Trench Town to St. Ann, going to the farm, and riding Nimble with that belly bouncing up and down under my chin.

But the clinic where I was being examined, in the village of Stepney, was quite a few miles away, and after a while I was so big, and it was so hard for me to walk any distance, that getting there became a problem. Then they said my iron was low and put me on some iron tablets. When I told Aunty, she had a fit. "See? You're not eating! What they're giving you? Only yam and cabbage! You have to come home, you have to drink milk, eat meat and fish, or you can't have the baby . . . Oh Lord, look what this child come to . . ."

And then I began to get nervous about the whole situation. I knew from what little I had studied in nursing school that some of what I needed was not available. And they'd just put a thermometer in someone's mouth, then maybe dip it in some alcohol and flash it and put it in your mouth! Getting closer to the time of Cedella's delivery, I began to think that Aunty's threats had some reason. "Because what if you should need a cesarean, or anything else should happen with this baby's delivery . . ." And oh no, I didn't want anything to happen to me or my baby, Bob's first baby. Besides, I'd begun to reconsider those warnings: What you gonna do down there? Gonna do farming? Gonna plant yams? I kept wondering where the decision to come here had taken me, apart from walking up and down the hill and going for water to the parish tank—which I enjoyed, but was this what I'd be doing for the rest of my life? After a while I began thinking about how I could make this change and not leave Bob, because I loved him so much that I wanted to be with him wherever he was going to be.

Eventually we decided that we should go back to Kingston a month before the baby was due. So I had Cedella in Kingston, and there we were, back at Aunty's again. But my brother had left the police force and emigrated to Canada, which made life a little easier because there was less tension in the house. And now we knew we had a place to go, that we could always go to St. Ann and be welcomed there. Most of all, even if it hadn't lasted, that taste of independence had been sweet.

After Cedella's birth, Sharon became the proud big sister, a role she very much enjoyed, and Aunty had two daughters to look after, which she loved because she could sew them pretty dresses. That was always her big thing, to make dresses for us, and she made a lot of them! Cedella and Sharon were the jewels in her crown, and as for me, her help was like a backbone. I could leave the kids to go out to work, because my working was as necessary for their welfare as staying home with them would have been. Even after six months away, there was still a demand for our music, so now that we were back in Kingston it was easy enough to pick up where we'd left off. Once we started working, we both felt better, and I began to understand even more clearly that music wasn't just something I had to do to feed us, but something that satisfied me the way nothing else ever would. (Though there were times when I thought I should try to go back to nursing just to save my family's face.)

After I got married, Marlene Gifford had left for New York, looking for her own life, because by then a little jealousy had started up. I guess she figured that because I was married and the mother of two, I might not need the Soulettes anymore, that the fun would be over. Shortly after she disappeared, Dream emigrated too, also to New York, to live with his brother Kenneth Smith and to get some schooling. Now Cecile Campbell and Hortense Lewis were singing with me, and this is when the Soulettes became triumphant characters. When we got to the three girls thing, we were hot—international musicians playing in Jamaica used us as an opening act, and we even went to Canada. Sometimes Bob would travel with us, like a security guard, to see our show and keep an eye on me. I loved it! We were busy—booked into various hotels and in demand for concerts. They called us "the Supremes of the Caribbean," and we were really kicking ass!

Cedella was about seven months old when Bob decided he'd had enough of staying at Aunty's. He felt like a parasite, he said, like a boy and not like the man he wanted to be at twenty-three. He felt he should take up his responsibilities and move his family out. He didn't feel free to express himself, to curse (he would never curse around Aunty). Besides, she had moved us from the main house and built a little one room for us at the front. And Bob said, you know what this means? Aunty herself wants us to go now. That was what he thought, of course; I myself wasn't so sure, since she was my right hand.

But I understood his position, and we decided to find a room with a shop. A room like ours at Aunty's, that was a shop by day and a bedroom at night, didn't work with children. Besides, though Bob thought having two daughters was great, he wanted a son (just like most Jamaican men do, it seems to me). So, with two babies and the prospect of another one soon, we began looking all over, and though it wasn't easy, we eventually found a room off Waltham Park Road with a shop front that adjoined it, where we could sell our records. It's amazing to me to look back at the person I was then. It's only now that I realize how young and inexperienced I was, going through all those changes and responsibilities and dealing with them quite normally. I'm surprised that I didn't wake up one morning and run away from it all!

But then things began to get a little complicated. The landlady found out who I was and then that Viola Britton was my aunt, and soon considered it her duty to report every action that took place in our rooms. Sometimes Bob and I actually got into physical fights, although it was like we were children, not in a "kill dead" fight but a love fight—the one you get into in order to make up. And I would fight! I wasn't going to take a blow, I was going to hit back—you hit me, I'm gonna hit you! I think Bob respected me for that. But though I was always the first to scratch, I'd start crying in a minute. And then, because he didn't like to see me cry, he would say, "Hey, that's not how we're supposed to live, I'm sorry" or "You made me do it," and things like that. And we would always make up before the night was over. I never let Aunty know, but she would look at me sometimes and say, "Uh-huh, you had a fight last night, I can tell" or "Why your face look like that?" or "What happened to your hand there?"

One night Bob and I had a fight because dinner was late. It was late because we didn't have a kitchen—I had to do the cooking on the ground in the doorway. Every morning and evening I had to catch a coal fire, fan it until it lit, and then wait for it to burn properly, which was hardly easy with one small baby not even sitting up yet and another still around my feet. The night we fought about the late dinner, Aunty's watchman got right on the job. As soon as she heard, Aunty came for me; she actually wanted to move me out, back to her house. And this was really a turnoff for Bob. "Am I not man enough to control my house?" he shouted. "Why can't I have a quarrel with my wife?"

But Aunty—so small but so powerful—said, "No, this is not what I sent her to school for!" And other things, because once again she thought I was being worthless. "When a man hits you, it's not good," she insisted. "It's a bad sign. So here it is, you're being mistreated, and this is not the life you're supposed to be living, this is not what I brought you up for!" And all of that and blah blah blah . . . So I let her take me back to her house. And then Bob came and he and I made up, of course. And Aunty, too.

At that time, the husband-wife thing seemed to me an unbreakable bond—you're bound to this relationship, you never think about getting out of it. Or you just have a commitment that you think, oh, this is going to be for the rest of my life, there's no way out. The vow alone was proof enough—for better for worse, for richer for poorer (for good or for bad, it seemed to me). Besides that, I was loving it and never thought, at that time, that this could ever end; I never thought Bob would leave me so soon and go to rest at the age of thirty-six. I never anticipated most of the things that happened because when I married, like most nineteen-year-old girls, I thought we were just going to be this way, love and happiness always. But marriage was a definite, real commitment to me, and added to it was that I always felt in sympathy with Bob and felt that I would always be his friend, come what may. It seemed more than a husband and wife thing with us; we were friends or, to look at it another way, despite whatever happened between us, we *decided* to be friends.

As for Aunty, and the question of where we would live, all that had to be put on hold, for the time being at least. Soon enough the new records the Wailers were making for Studio One as well as our own Wail'NSoul'M productions, and the airplay we got, made us stars again in Jamaica. The Wailers/Soulettes group began to go on little dates, overnight gigs to the North Coast, to Bournemouth Beach, to Cuba, and other Caribbean places like Gold Coast Beach in St. Thomas. And there was Aunty, who as always had my back, *was* my back, and who very agreeably became the nanny. No way could we have done what we did without her, and Bob, even with all his misgivings, knew this too, and loved her for being there for us.

But I realized, also, that I had taken up too much responsibility too soon. By the time I was twenty-two I had two children and still hadn't left Trench Town. I felt bad about the possibility of their growing up in an environment that didn't seem as if it was going to change. Poverty, corruption, violence—everything around us was the same as it had always been. Bob saw that I wasn't going to be laying back, accepting the situation as it was, accepting anything that happened, "I don't care, I'm gonna sleep today." How could I let this be my children's future?

No, I thought to that. Every day I'd say, "What's gonna be? What's gonna happen? Let's *make* something happen!" And I became what I guess you'd call a "quiet storm." On the surface you're smiling, but underneath you boil, and when you have to, you *roar.*

If you had been listening to Jamaican music in the late sixties, you'd have heard Burning Spear, Jimmy Cliff, Hortense Ellis, Marcia Griffiths, and certainly the Soulettes and the Wailers. One person with an ear out for all this was the American soul singer Johnny Nash, a frequent visitor to Jamaica who was looking for material for his company, JAD Records. In January 1967, at a Rastafarian religious ceremony, Rasta Elder Mortimo Planno introduced Nash to Bob, recommending him as "the best songwriter I know." Nash obviously agreed with Planno's assessment, because later he told his business partner, Danny Sims, that every one of the twenty-odd songs Bob played for him that night could be a hit.

Neville Willoughby, one of Jamaica's leading radio personalities, had also recommended Bob to Johnny Nash, so when Nash and Danny Sims came to Jamaica looking for us later that year, we were ready and interested. *Now,* we thought, *at last,* something good is going to happen. At that point we really needed something, because life seemed at a standstill: Sharon was still too young for school, Cedella was still in diapers (which I had to wash every day), and we were still at 18A Greenwich Park Road, all of us in that one little room at Aunty's. And soon there'd be more of us, because I was pregnant with my third child, hoping for the son we had asked Jah for.

Yet once again we had to thank Aunty, because at least we had a home with a veranda, where we could entertain these Americans. When they arrived, as usual she liked all the attention and excitement, and was happy to bring out drinks and crackers and cheese. And I had someone there to help me look after the children so I didn't have to feel pressured to be the singer, the hostess, and the mother all at once. After we started to work for JAD and began to see U.S. dollars for the first time, I said, "Aunty, see? Making good money now, good money coming in!" And so her story changed somewhat: Now when people asked about me she'd say, "Oh, she turned out not as we wanted, but t'ank god, she's not the *worst!*"

Americans can speak, they give you a picture on the wall that looks great. We were enticed by this prospect that our life was finally going to change. Here was what we'd been waiting for, people who could take us from one level to another. And at the beginning this seemed so true, because our initial meetings with the JAD people took place in a house that Johnny Nash owned, in the mountains overlooking Kingston in Russell Heights. Our first visits to—*oooohhh*, a house on the hilltop! Breathtaking!

Margaret Nash, Johnny's wife, befriended me right away. She was attracted to us but thought we were weird, she even said it right out: "You all are strange-looking people with your dreadlocks! And you're so quiet!" But I thought *she* was the quiet one. She was a very pretty, light-skinned woman with a lot of American Indian in her, and very kind, always looking out for me. I began to notice things, though, whenever I visited her house, things I hadn't ever seen before, and I realized that she was going through experiences I'd never even thought about. And I'm saying, wow, is this how Americans do it? Because Johnny would be in one room with girls, groupie kinds of girls, and Margaret would be in the next room talking business on the phone! And later I said to Bob, "Is this how married people live in America? This is Babylon life! This is Babylon life, Bob," I kept insisting. "Do you see what they're doing?" I was really shocked and vowed never to get caught up in that way of living. I felt very insecure and skeptical about the whole situation, and I worried about what we were getting into, even as I was drawn to it all. I liked the next level and certainly the dollars, but I felt that as Rastafarians we should be careful about this kind of exposure.

One day they wanted a photo session, and when I arrived Margaret said, "Oh no, that's not how we want you, Rita! You're too young and beautiful, you need to dress up, we want to see your strong legs!" So she gave me a minidress, one of hers, and oh! To my surprise, I was so excited to be in that dress! By then my hair was in a short Afro, and after Margaret gave me some earrings to go with the minidress she put me in front of a mirror and said, "Look! This is you! Look how pretty you are, look how pretty you are!"

And I looked. I hadn't seen myself that way for a long while, not since I was seventeen or eighteen. After that I'd been really into being a true Rasta sister. And maybe I relaxed, right there. I guess I understood that there was part of me that hadn't changed, that wouldn't change no matter what I wore. Because I still felt like a true Rasta sister. Maybe that's why I appreciated Margaret's encouragement so much, her always reminding me how pretty I was and always watching out for me amongst the men. Whenever she thought I seemed tired, she'd say, "Oh, you have to come in and lie down on my bed. You can't keep up with these guys, Rita, you're pregnant!"

Because "these guys" would be strumming guitar from six in the evening until six in the morning. And I'd be there thinking, wow, we're really in this now, and wondering how do they do it? Then Danny Sims would pass out things he called "vitamins." I didn't even realize it at the time, but those vitamins were uppers—yes, uppers! That's what we found out later!

And I'm saying what a wicked man, this is so dangerous! He could have killed my baby!

That baby, my third, was a home delivery, born in Trench Town in our little room in Aunty's compound. We had decided not to go back to the public hospital with this one; we figured we could save money by just having the village midwife come by, since it wasn't as if I was inexperienced. I forget where Bob was when I went into labor—somewhere but not far. Aunty, having prepared Bob for the experience, left to send someone to tell him, and when she returned she said, "He is going to help with this one, let him see the pain! Let him see the pain, let him see!"

When he arrived, she said to him, "Robbie, you feel up to it?"

And he said, very definitely, "Yes, Aunty!"

"Okay, you can help then," she said. "Just give me a drink." And he got her a drink of Wincarnis, a beer for himself, and thyme tea for me, and they called the midwife. And of course there I was with no anesthesia, *ooh, ah, ooh*, in pain, until the midwife came and announced, "She's ready!"

At that point Aunty said to Bob, "You go dig a hole in the yard, because we're going to have to put the afterbirth in it. And get the water and more newspaper! Come, come! Move fast, she's in hard pain!"

Poor Bob! I looked at him and he was so . . . pale! Poor Bob—he looked like *he* was going to have the baby! But we kept our eyes on each other, and in the end he was very much a part of the delivery. And when he saw that the baby was a boy, *oooh!* He went outside to his friends and I heard noise, and when he came back in he was so uplifted! He couldn't stop smiling, and he was so proud—all night you could hear him telling his friends, "I have a son, man! I have a son! A boy! A boy! A boy!"

And later, after Aunty and the midwife and the helpers had cleaned up, and everyone had gone home, he begged Aunty, "Can I sleep on the bed tonight, with Rita and the baby? Will that be all right?"

Aunty by this time was pleased with him, because he really had been helpful, and she was touched by his excitement. "Of course," she said, but then added, "As long as you're clean!"

I said, "Oh, Aunty, you know Bob is clean!"

"Yeah," he agreed, but then just to be sure, he said, "If that is the case, let me go bathe." So he went outside and took a shower. And when he came to bed we named the baby David, for King David, of course, though he became known as Ziggy, a pet name Bob himself had once had, and which he gave the baby three days later, saying he had football legs. Ziggy describes a move by a football (soccer) player who can outmaneuver everyone on the field.

At the time our work with JAD began, Bunny had been incarcerated for marijuana use, so most of the demo tapes we made consisted of Bob and me and sometimes Peter Tosh. When we finally did sign a contract, I would be in the studio for *hours*. We worked in Jamaica until JAD got us passports and visas to travel to the United States. We got tickets for ourselves and the children to Wilmington, Delaware, where we planned to stay a while with Bob's mother and her family before leaving for New York. To the children it was a dream come true to be to going to see Grandma and her husband Eddie Booker, and their Aunt Pearl and uncles Richard and Anthony, none of whom they'd met. Going to see Bob's family and going to school in America! (At that time Cedella Booker was running a nursery, a day care center for children, and ours were to be part of it, so that I would be able to go to work.) So that was a catch! And a new experience for the kids and me, moving to America.

But then we wondered how it was going to work and if it was going to work at all. What kind of decision was this, to pack up and go? My position, and I said it more than once, was that this move must be for the better. We could not be in the situation we were in now, in Jamaica with three kids and still not seeing any future in the music business. And this hand-to-mouth thing was getting out of order.

On the flight to Delaware Bob was such a good father. Assisting with diaper changing, feeding bottles, everything. I don't know what I'd have done without his help, because that was an experience, flying with three children! After arriving and going through customs—another ordeal with three children—we sat down in the terminal, waiting to be picked up. Moments later, Ziggy, who was still nursing, wanted to be fed. So I took out my breast and started to feed him. Bob had gone somewhere and was on his way back to us when he saw me doing this—and he got so upset! "Why are you doing that?" he said. "Cover up yourself—you don't do that in America!"

Now it was my turn to be upset! I said, "What are you talking about?"

"How could you do that?" he said. "You know, if my mother saw you doing that she would never . . . In America you can't feed the baby like that! You go one side or maybe go in the toilet!"

I couldn't believe it. That seemed absurd—to feed your baby in the *toilet!* I said, "Come on now, Bob, that's nothing. My baby's hungry, and when my baby's hungry I'll feed my baby anywhere!" A few years later women in the States actually had to demonstrate for the right to nurse their babies in public.

When Cedella and Eddie Booker arrived, they couldn't imagine how we'd managed, with the children and the baggage and everything else, because in addition to all that I'd brought all the Jamaican foods I knew Mrs. Booker had been craving—roast breadfruit, ackee, mango, tea bush, every little thing. She kept saying, "How did you do it? How did you do this?" And she couldn't believe her eyes when she took a good look at me, she said, because I looked exactly like her when she was young! Later, when we put our faces together, people said to her, "Is Rita your child or is Nesta?" (Like the rest of Bob's family, she called him Nesta.) And I began to understand why he might have loved me so. Maybe he was really looking for a replacement after she left him and went to America, and when he saw me, resembling her so much yet as ambitious as he himself was, he might have thought, *ooh*, this is what I need, this is *my* girl.

That was Bob's favorite song when he was trying to catch my attention: "My girl, my girl/ She used to be my girl . . ." He would sing it whenever he came in: "She used to be *my* girl, she used to be *my* girl . . ." Hearing it, I'd know he had something up his sleeve. We had a normal lifestyle, with our secret little ways of communicating like any other young couple. The only difference was the chance that music gave us. It was a treasure to us, a gift, but we didn't *expect* things, we didn't have any great plans or fantasies about what we'd do if we got rich and famous. Superstardom was far from our minds; we were simply trying to establish ourselves and to become independent in the only way that seemed open to us.

After a short time in Wilmington, we left the children with Eddie and Moms (as I eventually called Cedella Booker) and took the train to New York. I have to admit I was scared. When we got off the train in New York and headed for Johnny and Margaret Nash's apartment, where we were staying, I was almost afraid to walk along the street. I kept saying, "I don't like those buildings, they look like they're going to fall over anytime! They're too tall! I won't look up—that's Babylon and it's going to crumble!" But everyone said, no man, it's okay. Still, after I got over my fear, I was so impressed that it was hard for me to believe what I was seeing. This was *America*. Everything seemed so perfect, from the sidewalks to the storefronts to the clothing people wore. And the guest room in Johnny and Margaret 's place—that first night, when Bob and I had sex, we didn't want to mess up the bed, so we did it on the table in the kitchen!

In Jamaica, when Margaret had found out that we would be coming to New York, she'd been all excited at the prospect. "Girl, when I get my hands on you, I'm gonna dress you *up!*" she had promised. As soon as I got there this became necessary, because it was winter and I was definitely not dressed for forty degrees. Even if I had known what to expect, I couldn't have afforded to prepare for it in any case. So the very next day after we arrived Margaret took me shopping. She took me uptown—I remember her emphasizing that: "Rita, I'm gonna take you *uptown*, girl!"

On the way there, I kept my eyes open. To my surprise, I began to see people who looked like me, more black people around. And it started to dawn on me that there was a lot I didn't know about America. Apart from what we picked up from movies, this was also what America looked like. There were people sitting in the street, I even saw beggars on the sidewalk and homeless people around. In America! I'd thought this was only in Trench Town. I suppose Margaret took me uptown not only to shop, but for many different reasons—especially to expose me to the fact that even if I was out of one ghetto, here we were in the Big Apple, in another (though I liked it).

In the course of the afternoon she dressed me from top to bottom, including a coat, stockings, and shoes. Then she took me somewhere else, where a woman taught me about makeup and shaped my Afro. Then we went back to Margaret's apartment, and she prettied me up some more. I think she was just as excited as I was, because I remember her saying, at one point, "You know, we gonna really show them something!" Then we went to the studio, and Bob was astonished! "Ah, Margaret!" he said, accusingly. "What have you done to Rita?" Not only was I wearing different clothes, I even had on eyebrow pencil, something I'd never before worn (and seldom have since)!

So I had a new look, and even after three children I had a new interest too from Mr. Marley. Later, when we were alone, he took a long look at me and said, "Wow, so you went and got yourself a fresh face!"

It's many years since then, but I'm still thanking Margaret for that face.

Back then, all the magazine stories I'd read as a girl had said that when you got married it was understood that you were going to be married for life, you were going to be devoted. Even though my mother and father had split up, Aunty had divorced Mr. Britton, and Cedella Booker had had her trials, I was sure—maybe because I was so young—that my relationship with Bob would last. True, I would sometimes make arguments, usually about his flirting with other women, sometimes really just to pick a fight or even threaten him: "I think I'm gonna live somewhere else and stay away from you." (But then I would start crying.)

When we got to New York, though, a new element was added, because it was a record company recommendation that you shouldn't let your fans know you were married. How could you be a devoted husband and sell records? I didn't know this until I read, in a newspaper interview: "Bob, we hear you're married—is it true you're married to Rita?" And his answer was, "Oh no, she's my sister!"

I waited until the next time we were alone to question him about it. That night we were sitting in the living room, looking out at the lights of New York. I had the newspaper on the table, ready. I went over to him and put it in his hand.

"Oh, I saw that," he said. He didn't seem interested. Maybe he was thinking about something else.

"Yes, but what does this mean? Why you tell the press we're not married?"

"Oh that's just show business," he said. "But then, who wants to expose you? You're mine!"

I must not have looked satisfied, because he stood up and took my hand in his. "Listen, man," he said. "Just cool." That was his favorite expression, "Just cool."

"Because look at this," he went on. "Let me show you something." And he pulled me to him, until we were facing each other quite close, almost close enough to kiss. We loved to kiss, kissing was one of our main functions! So I said to myself, *uh-oh,* he's gettin' ready to kiss me now and there I go . . . there I go . . . there I go . . .

But this time he was drawing something in the palm of his hand, showing me a circle. "Listen, Rita," he said. "You see this circle, this is like life, where we have to go around different places and meet different people. But inside this circle, this is where we are, you and me. And you see this line that go around it? Nobody can break that line to come into the circle with you and me, it's protected. This is me, this is you, this is the children, all the important people are inside this ring. Anything happens outside it doesn't have a proper meaning, and nothing can get inside. So don't worry yourself, man, you're safe, you're my queen, my wife, my life."

From then on I felt all right, reassured and very special, because Bob was genuine in the ways he expressed himself. And it was also like him to know I needed that confidence and to give it to me. So I learned to ignore the follies that happened around me, to tell myself, oh, they don't matter. That's how I felt. And I felt, given Bob's increasingly recognized genius, that I'd become more like a guardian—a friend, a partner—than in a possessive relationship, and that I had more responsibility than just that of a wife. This attitude would get me through the more difficult times that came later, when the "sister" thing had gone further than I'd ever expected. But I always had myself somewhere in mind, and when anyone came at me with "Bob says you're his sister—is that true?" I'd come back with "Yes, I'm his sister. And I'd rather be a good sister than a miserable wife."

One interesting result of the association with JAD Records was Bob's trip to Europe, which included a purely accidental meeting with my father. Danny Sims had taken Bob to Sweden to record the soundtrack for a movie, *Want So Much to Believe* (in which, as it turned out, none of Bob's original songs were ever used). Bob hated cold weather, but he had moved to the cold basement of the house where Johnny Nash's entourage was staying in order to get away from their lifestyle—the drugs, the whores, everything he disapproved of. He told me later that he thought he was going to die of the cold and had said to himself, if I'm gonna die, let me die in the basement—because they were eating pork upstairs, and cooking this and that, and *oh* . . . poor Bob. He was going through a hard time, having no friends there and no one to talk to. Someone made a tape of him in a bedroom there, singing solo with just his acoustic guitar. Especially on "Stir It Up," I can hear all that loneliness in him: "Stir it up, little darlin'/stir it up/It's been a long long time/since I've had you on my mind . . ."

I suppose that's why it seems like such a miracle that he and my father got together. I think they both thought so too (in later years Papa used to tell this story over and over). At the time, Papa was working as a taxi driver and playing music in Stockholm. One night a friend, knowing where Papa was from, said to him, "A young man came in from Jamaica man, a young man named Bob Marley. He's somewhere in town with that American, Johnny Nash."

And Papa said, "What?! Bob *Mah*-ley? Bob Mah-*ley*! But that name sound familiar! I think my daughter's husband name Mahley! Let me see the guy, man!" So he got in touch with the person who was doing the cooking for Johnny Nash and said, "Let me meet this guy *Mah*-ley, man. Tell him Rita father coming." And when Papa arrived, Bob came up from the basement. And there was my father, saying, "Yes, man, Rita is my daughter. You married to my daughter!"

Bob said it was like heaven—it was a release, as if he'd gotten out of prison, a prison term in a Stockholm basement! His letter said, "Guess what? I met your father, and he's teaching me to play some new stuff on the guitar!" Bob said he could hardly believe it had happened—and purely by chance. From then on, Papa would come in the evenings and take him out for food and a smoke, and their relationship grew. It was my father who taught Bob some techniques of the classic guitar, things that he himself had learned after emigrating, which helped Bob to write to a more advanced level and to experiment with better chords. I remember when

I got that letter I was so happy! I wrote Bob, "Here I've been suffering and wondering what's happening to you, and there you are, hanging out with my Papa!"

Working with JAD, I had stopped acting as the sales manager and had become just a singer, even though Bob and I were bound in a "keep your eyes open, we're going to sign contracts" understanding. But then we started meeting lawyers and accountants, and anyway I couldn't be in the studio and out there selling records too. Still, we found out soon enough that JAD was covering Wailers' music—"Stir It Up" was a big hit for them, and "Guava Jelly," which Barbra Streisand also covered. JAD used Bob's capacity as a songwriter, but they wanted to make a star of Johnny Nash, not of Bob Marley, and Bob Marley wanted to be his own self, the person he had a vision of himself becoming. We were getting only minimum royalties, because they had everything set up so that they owned the publishing, the copyright, and all that.

Just before the association with JAD was over, Bob found himself stranded in London with Peter and Bunny. After Bob's stint in Stockholm, Danny Sims had sent for the two other Wailers with some idea that he could promote them by sending them on tour in England. They played a few dates but nothing more happened, and one morning they woke up in their cold-water flat to find they'd been abandoned altogether—Nash and Sims had left for Florida. Bob managed to make a connection that would later serve them all well, but as things stood then, they got the plane fare home, and that was that.

Little or none of the material recorded as demos for JAD was released during Bob's lifetime, but the market was flooded with it after he passed. We had been so inexperienced, and lacking proper guidance or preparation, that we'd been misled. So at the time we just marked JAD as an experience that had in any case been good for us.

But then it was over; the contract was up. We didn't know how long it would be before a new contract came along, or that we would wait out some more hard times before the world began to take notice. When it did, though, it embraced Robert Nesta Marley. I was to sing with him for the last, most successful, years of his life. Apart from our personal relationship, working with him was always new, always interesting. Everyone who ever did agrees to this. As a good friend once said, Bob was "one of a kind and truly a prophet sent . . . I didn't wait until he passed to give him flowers."

chapter six
A TIME TO TURN

I DON'T LIKE TO remember the summer of 1971, it was such a low time. Of course I was glad to see Bob when he came home; I'd been lonely and worried. In those days you couldn't just pick up a phone, you had to stand by the gate and wait for the postman (though with three children to care for, I didn't have much time for standing and waiting). Still, whenever I wasn't working, *doing* something, I was back to asking myself, is this all there is? Is this what my life is gonna be? What kind of future am I making for myself and my children?

As soon as Bob returned, the Wailers went into Coxsone's studio. I wasn't singing background vocals for them at that time, so I had no income and nothing to do but worry. Bob wasn't earning any money either, although he was working hard on a deal that he hoped for. We were getting some small checks from JAD and had managed to buy a little used car, but the music thing was definitely not working. Our records were not playing in America or even in Jamaica. And of course we were still at Aunty's, which put me back into my childhood position, as though I'd never grow up and would always be dependent. My kids now used the stool that Papa had made for me.

And then I discovered I was pregnant. The day I knew, I took that stool to the corner of the yard where I used to go after Aunty's spankings and sat there trying to absorb this latest calamity and to figure out what to do. I was devastated; I couldn't imagine how this would affect everyone. As a strict Rastafarian I did not use birth control or believe in abortion; it's our belief that such practices are intended to kill off the black race.

I waited as long as I could before making the big announcement. I told myself this was "just to be sure," but that was just an excuse. Aunty's response was predictable. She stood with her hands on her hips and her nose in the air, saying, "My Lord, what is this? Again? Not another baby! I knew it was gonna happen, you can't go on like this, you've got to put a stop, you have to find a place to put your children! No more in here! This is going crazy! Where is the money coming from? What are you doing with your life? You cannot stay here with so many children! There's no room—everybody is in one room and that's not right. You never grow that way, you grow with your own room. To have so many kids in one room? No!"

I knew that everything she'd said was true, and her talking like this really got to me. For the first time I really understood how this new situation of ours, this complete dependency, was too much for her. Bob was more sympathetic when I told him, but he was overwhelmed with career problems. We talked it over that night and I asked if he thought I could call his mother, maybe I would go to the States for a while, until he got himself out of the troubles he was in, his commitment to a record deal with JAD that was not working for us. Then maybe he could come up there and join me.

So he agreed that I should call, and I decided that even if I didn't go to America, I'd move out anyway. I had to get away from Aunty. I didn't want her to see me growing a big belly again. Bob and I had actually been looking for houses but had been turned away time and again because of the children. So the more I thought about it, going to Delaware seemed like a good idea. I told Bob I would get a job. "I don't know what I'll do, but I'll do something," I said. "I'll do nursing, housework, whatever it takes, and you'll stay, and I'll send whatever money I can manage to send for you and the kids."

So I got in touch with Moms Booker, who said yes, you can come and stay with me until Bob can get here (she was very pleased about that). My plan, as I explained to her, was to come to Delaware and get back into practical nursing. I didn't want to leave Sharon and Cedella, but they were both in school and I thought it would be wiser not to arrive with everyone, so I took Ziggy and Aunty agreed to keep the girls. Leaving them was hard, but there just wasn't room in Delaware at that time. On bad days it seemed as if there wasn't room for us anywhere.

It was winter when I got to Wilmington. I got work immediately in a hospital as a nurse's aide, but such a low-paying job couldn't pay my expenses—the rent I had to give to the Bookers, and what Moms charged me for babysitting Ziggy, and what I was trying to save to send back home to Aunty and Bob. Every day I wished he would hurry up and get over here, because this was a different kind of life.

But Eddie Booker was a sweet man and so devoted to his "Ciddy"—I used to love just watching them in love. Eddie was much older than his wife, and when he heard her calling him—heard that "Eddie!"—he just smiled. He'd been a bit overwhelmed by us during the Johnny Nash period, when he knew that we were actually working with an American. It was a big deal to him, and he'd state so proudly, "Oh, they're signed to this American man from New York!" and "Yes, Ciddy's son is a singer, and his wife is also a singer!" And he had really embraced Bob's writing. He'd even fixed up the basement so we could have that to ourselves, because he knew we smoked, and they didn't like us to smoke in the house.

When I was there alone with Ziggy, what impressed me about their family and what really got me hooked at first was that every evening Eddie took us all for a ride. Pearl, the big sister, was about thirteen, and Richard and Anthony were a few years younger. Every evening Eddie would have a sip of his Coke, and light a cigarette, and then we either had to go get a "sub" or go for a ride—"Ciddy, where we going this evening, Ciddy?" And it was always somewhere far, a couple of hours' ride, and we'd come back when all the kids had fallen asleep. For me this was so relaxing, and so much fun, and it made me happy to see Ziggy enjoying the big kids and this real, picture-perfect "family outing." Another family member—Bob's cousin Dotty, whom I'd first met in St. Ann—was living in Wilmington and she really looked out for me as well.

But it soon reached the point where I had to do housework as well as nursing. I had various jobs, and then got one as a live-in nurse-housekeeper for a very old woman, whose wealthy children let her live by herself. Maybe they couldn't stand her, or maybe she preferred this, although from what I could see, she was miserable. But she owned a mansion, and that's where we lived, just the two of us.

Working for Mrs. Carrington was a task, and frightening, because although aged she could be scary. So was the neighborhood, where only rich white people lived, and the only black people I ever saw were the maids. It gave me a weird feeling when I thought about it, that I was a helper now, a maid. If I sometimes snuck a phone call, I would have to listen to Mrs. Carrington going over her bill: "Who made this call? That damn *maid*!" Old as she was, she would inspect her silver with a magnifier to be sure I had cleaned it properly and count it to be sure I had not stolen any on my day off.

After Mrs. Carrington had her morning coffee, and maybe toast and scrambled eggs, she didn't eat again until two or three o'clock, when she would pick out what she wanted for dinner. She counted everything—each slice of bread (and you could only have one), each egg. She measured all our food by the spoon, never a measuring cup. For the two of us she'd dole out maybe two to five spoonfuls of whatever we were eating, or one lamb chop and one baked potato—for us both, and that was it for the night! So I'd find myself many nights, after I put her to bed, sneaking down to the kitchen to steal an egg or a chop, even a piece of bread or a potato, because I was always hungry—and not just because I was pregnant, though that certainly had something to do with it. Thinking about this now, I realize I've really had a life . . .

But even more than the hunger, and the fear and embarrassment involved in stealing food, what I minded was the loneliness. My room was in the attic, and there wasn't all that much work to do. I missed home—not only Bob and my girls but Jamaica itself, with its sunshine and music. I missed Ziggy, whom I was able to see only on my weekend off. Sometimes I'd cry myself to sleep, other times I swore I heard ghosts in that cold, empty house. Just the silence of the place alone would drive me crazy. But I stuck it out—and Mrs. Carrington was even going to sponsor me to the United States, I was told, if I stayed on as a live-in. So I guess I was a good enough maid.

I kept waiting for Bob to come to Delaware, but then he got a draft notice from the U.S. government. It was the time of the Vietnam War, and because he had taken out citizenship papers, they wanted him for military service. The letter said, essentially, "We got you!" But Bob's response was, "No, I'm gonna run." So there was no more talk of his joining me. And at the same time he would not give up on his music. So each day he would write two or more songs about, as usual, his life—for example: "Talking Blues," "My Woman Is Gone," "Baby Come on Home."

Caught up there in Mrs. Carrington's attic, with no end in sight, I had a lot of time to think. Something in me still couldn't believe that this was it, that this was where I'd remain. I fooled myself into believing that what I was going through was just to keep my independence, and that things weren't going to be this way always. And then sometimes—just when I needed him, it seemed—Bob would call to give me encouragement, to say again, "Just cool, soon everything will be fine, either you come back to Jamaica or whatever, but don't stay there and worry yourself."

It was sweet Eddie Booker who gave me the most immediate hope. Just before my weekend off, he'd call to say, "Oh Rita, I'm coming to get you!" And he'd drive me home and oh, I was so glad to see my boy Ziggy! But then one day it was snowing, and when I got home I found that Ziggy had been playing in the park across the street with some kids who'd thrown snow inside his jacket. He came down with pneumonia and I had to rush him to the hospital that night, one of his lungs almost collapsed. I nearly died, I cried so, I kept saying, "No no no, I can't leave Ziggy anymore, 'cause they're gonna kill him." Things were getting out of hand now, I thought, I think it's time for me to go, this would never have happened around Aunty. I called Bob, and said, "I'm coming home."

He said, "It don't make sense to come home, there's nothing to come home for because nothing is happening in Jamaica."

I was so upset. What had happened to "Just cool—soon everything will be fine"? I knew I'd have to have the new baby in Delaware if I couldn't come home right then, because I was almost due, and soon it would be too late to fly. A kind of uncertainty crept in about Bob that I'd never felt before. I realized we're separating, we're growing apart. What's happening here?

So I said, "As soon as I can, after this baby is born, since you're not coming to America, I'm coming home. And that's it."

I worked right up to the time the baby was due. I had to. So that if anyone said, "Your child is eating a lot!" I could say, "No problem." I'd get my pay, pay this, help out that, buy everybody a beer, and we'd drink and be happy. But living with Cedella Booker was an experience. Soon after Ziggy's pneumonia I'd left Mrs. Carrington to work days in the hospital, and so I was home to take care of Moms at night—bathe her, oil her hair. She looked forward to that, it was my "daughter-in-law thing." We would sit and watch TV and I would be there for hours, chatting, making her comfortable, before we went to bed. But the time I spent with her was great; I learned a lot from Moms, so I didn't mind so much that I had to wash out her tub after bathing her and other things daughters-in-law don't do anymore. And then sometimes at night I had to scrub her kitchen floor, and wax it, so that in the morning it would be shiny when she went down to make Eddie's coffee and bologna sandwiches for her boys' school lunch.

Sometimes I was able to speak to Sharon and Cedella if Aunty took them to the post office to get a connection to call me in Delaware. I'd listen to their little voices asking, "Mommy, when are you coming home?" and I would end up in tears. At night I'd try to sneak out of the house to smoke a little spliff or end up sobbing myself to sleep. I don't know how I did it those last few months. I must have been so strong even though back then I felt so weak.

The only relief I had from all the Delaware pressure was an occasional trip to Brooklyn, where my father was living with Alma Jones. The first time things got truly uncomfortable and I felt I had to run away, I called Papa and he said, "Just take the train." As if it were so easy! Although I'd been on the train before when we were working with JAD, I felt unsure of myself now, especially with my big belly and Ziggy still a little boy. It was Eddie Booker, that sweet soul, who took me to the train station, got my ticket, and saw me off. He made sure I was on the right train and cautioned me, "Don't get off till you hear them say, 'New York, New York'!"

It was a five-hour ride, at least, and Ziggy usually fell asleep, so I could just relax and stare out the window and think. At the time Cedella Booker didn't recognize the faith of Rastafari, though she has since become more interested. So between us there was always some general warfare about that, besides "I have to get home to clean the kitchen." Sometimes my trips to New York would follow pleas for backup money to my cousin

Kenneth, with whom Dream had lived for a while; other times I'd just sit on the phone crying to Papa, or Miss Alma, "Oh, we had a fight" or "Mrs. Booker's barking at me again." And they'd say, come up here for the weekend, come to Brooklyn.

Today, when I see young women who look like me, who seem to be living that same life, I look at them and remember how I used to feel then. How I used to get off the railroad, find the right subway to get to the house, pregnant me and the little boy Ziggy, in the middle of winter. Feeling so tired and lost but so upright and determined, until I'd buzz that door and a voice said, "Who is it?" and I'd say, "It's Rita!" and Miss Alma would scream and then come running down the eight flights of steps to get us, crying, "And the baby, how you come in such cold!" Oh, she'd make a fuss, and then the sweetest rice and peas, with oxtail, Papa's favorite dish. And, surprisingly, I began to understand my father in a way I never had before. It was amazing to me how many little jobs I'd seen him trying to do, to keep on being a musician and make a living—in London, Stockholm, and now Brooklyn. Right then, his children with Miss Alma, George and Margaret, as well as Kingsley, Papa's adopted son, were living in England with Miss Alma's sister. And I realized that although I'd been angry at him when he left me with Aunty, he was only trying to support his family, which he had hardly ever managed to do.

But whenever I ran away to New York and came back there was a big quarrel. "Why you have to go to see your father, why, what news did you take to them?" I felt as trapped then as Bob had been in Stockholm with Johnny Nash. And I couldn't blame Bob because he was trying, too. I guess because we were so young and inexperienced we were not able to support each other morally, to say, well, this is life, it's coming at us in a way we didn't expect. We were lucky enough to have families who put up with us and helped us when we needed them.

Our second son, Stephen, was born in April. I went back to work in the hospital right away, figuring I'd work and try to save some money until he was about five months old, although I really wanted to go home right then. But one night, after an incident I can't even remember (there were so many), I went into my room, sat on the bed, took out my writing paper, and sat there for a while thinking of what to say. I was so tired I could barely hold the pen. The house was very quiet. "Dear Aunty," I wrote, "I think I'm being taken advantage of." I realized that not only was I homesick, I was really getting too tired to go on this way, working so hard and not ever feeling happy, and wondering all the time about what Bob was doing and what was happening in Jamaica. Although the Bookers tried to make me feel comfortable, and Moms especially, for Bob's sake, didn't want me to feel as if I was not accepted as part of the family, there was just too much pressure. And I thought I'd had enough of America.

When Aunty got my letter, she called, saying, "Oh my God, what's going on?" The Bookers were concerned, Moms very upset that I'd written my family that kind of letter. Then I found out that in Jamaica there was more trouble: Bob was still living with Aunty and the two girls, yet there'd be nights he didn't come home, although that was "home"—where they washed his clothes and he came for dinner (when he wanted to, since I wasn't there). Aunty was even more miserable than she'd been before I left, because her expectations weren't being in any way fulfilled. It seemed to her that Bob was getting less ambitious, because he took sides with his boys and didn't have a job.

He had said all along that he was going to stay in Jamaica to see what would happen with the connection he had made in London, that he was going toward something. But he was miserable, too, and before anything happened with the music a lot of fooling around went on that had nothing to do with music. I think men have less patience than women; if they try something and it doesn't work, they immediately get upset with themselves that they didn't do the right thing. Women tend to think first how it's going to affect us, the children—in other words, we're left with the responsibility.

. . .

I went home as soon as Stephen could sit up. I didn't know until then about the two young women Bob had been seeing while I was in Delaware, though I had suspected one even before I'd left—I'd even gone to her mother to say, "Tell your daughter to stay away from my husband!" Both of these women had become pregnant at the same time, their sons born about a month after Stephen. I was very upset at first to learn about all this, though it's common in Jamaica. But since then, I've come to love both of these boys and to think of them as my sons.

I had a little money saved. When I found out about this new situation, my first thought was that I needed to stand on my own two feet. Even though I still loved Bob, and was glad to see him and for the time being wanted to remain his wife, I realized I couldn't completely trust this man anymore with my life and my children. I really had to try to forget about him for a while—even if that was hard to do—and focus on the four children: Sharon, Cedella, Ziggy, and now Stephen.

First thing, I'd seek after getting out of Trench Town, however I could make that happen. It seemed crucial. I felt especially bad for Ziggy, who had been going to school in Delaware and was accustomed to certain treatment—it was a new life in Trench Town. I was only twenty-five, but I felt I'd achieved a degree of knowledge and experience and wanted some respect. I had worked too hard in Delaware and felt I should *use* whatever I'd gained, not just financially but morally. I'm gonna give something to my children, I thought, these kids are too nice, I owe it to them. And if Bob doesn't want to be part of it, too bad. I felt as if I had something to boast about—even though I had nothing except a few American dollars that would soon be gone.

Of course Aunty said, "You crazy? What you gonna be doing? Ah, Robbie not makin' one bit a money and you come back? Why you never stay in America? What you come for? Why you followin' *him*?" She thought I should divorce him.

But I thought this was not for a Rasta to do, not a good example. So even though I was in so much pain, I said no, he's still my husband and I don't want to lose my husband. I asked myself, can I hold out? I knew he loved the kids as much as I did, but that he was distracted because of all the pressures, there was just too much mix-up. Where there's weakness I have to be strong, I thought. I have to be strong for the kids. Even if I'm angry as hell at Bob, I have to be strong for him. I felt I had to take the lead, and that we had to try to be friends because we were partners now, we were connected forever, we were family.

chapter seven
THANK YOU, JAH

WHATEVER FEW DOLLARS I brought home from Delaware blew in a couple of weeks, because I had to go up to Courts and take out a double bed and an extra dresser for the kids. It almost seemed as if I'd turned back the clock by coming home. Once again we were living hand to mouth, with neither of us working and the JAD royalties nearly nonexistent. Nothing had changed, and only trouble had been added.

When Bob returned from London after the JAD thing fell apart, he'd said, "Well, a man named Chris Blackwell is coming to Jamaica, you'll soon see here, Rita, things might work out, there might be a deal." And so forth . . . But that to me had been just a big maybe, and I didn't know much about Chris; in any event, there had been no money.

These days, the name Chris Blackwell is widely known, since his company, Island Records, has been responsible for taking Jamaican music to the rest of the world. Chris grew up in Jamaica, in an Anglo-Jamaican family, and by the time Bob walked into his London office he had been promoting Caribbean music for more than a decade. In Jamaica he'd already established a small record label, Blue Mountain/Island, and in 1962, when he moved to London, he began to release recordings by performers like Millie Small, Jimmy Cliff, and the Skatalites. Chris had even reissued some of the Wailers' early work for Coxsone, recorded under the name Wailing Wailers. This was what led them—stranded in London—to look him up. It was Chris's interest and belief in the Wailers, and in Jamaican music in general, that had sent Bob and Bunny and Peter home on the plane with a promise: Bring me an album and we'll see what we can do.

Not long after I returned from Delaware, just when I was beginning to doubt anything would ever happen, Chris made the Wailers an offer. He was going against advice: He'd been told that he was crazy to even think he could get a deal with them, that they were not to be trusted and would surely rip him off—"You don't put your money on these guys, they're the rude boys! You may never see them again!" But Chris had had earlier, positive experiences with Rastafarians that led to his interest, and he really had his finger on the pulse of Jamaican music. And I think he had the same reaction to the Wailers that I myself had at first. From the day I met them I saw *something* about them that was different from ordinary Trench Town bad boys—there was some class to them, some future. Chris has said that "something about them" made him feel as if he could trust them, maybe the way they delivered themselves. And now they had delivered. So he decided to give them money to go into the studio.

And this is where everybody started to smile—there was no deal so far, but a deal was clearly in sight. I felt some relief, as if I could breathe again, and I even began to get along better with Aunty because we could help out with money to buy food, and I knew I could soon get out of her house. Chris was also making it easy for the music to happen. In the early seventies he had bought a large, run-down house at 56 Hope Road, uptown near Jamaica House, the prime minister's residence, and also near Devon House, a landmark mansion where his mother had been raised. The place, which he named Island House, included some acreage and a few outbuildings in the back. It was shabby but livable. Chris set it up as a gathering/rehearsal space for the musicians he wanted to promote, and in short order he and Bob arranged that after the release of the first album, Bob was to take over the property, giving him a place to hold interviews and press conferences. As things worked out, eventually the ownership of 56 Hope Road passed to Bob, as a final payment for his share of the three-album deal the Wailers signed.

When all this started, Bob was of course thrilled. He kept saying to me, "Listen, we'll have a house!" As for me, I was astonished, especially by the location—ordinarily, if you didn't have money or you weren't white (or brown), you could hardly set foot in that area. Plus a Rasta! Even worse! Hope Road was the first time any such achievement had ever happened to a Rasta. To be able to flash dreadlocks and wear the Rastafarian colors in a home beside the governor general's—the king's house! A home beside the prime minister's place where he has his office—two doors from it! Right in the limelight, in the middle of uptown!

And so there was a big amazed buzz in the community when the Wailers took the place over. Chris himself usually stayed elsewhere, but Bob, Peter, and Bunny and a number of others were regulars. About moving there myself, I felt apprehensive. I wasn't that enthused, although I was happy that things were working out for us. Still, I didn't feel as if it would be *my* house. After all, there were three Wailers, and they were partners, and whatever the deal was, everybody had to be sharing. And even while pushing for the house, Bob wasn't giving me the motivation: He never said, "Hey, Rita, come on, move the kids." I just wasn't getting that *zeal*. Whenever I was there, I could see that it was more of a group thing, because not only were the Wailers there, but other people as well, and girls, and . . . *things* were going on. I could see that Chris was using Island House as a sort of catch for Bob: You can have your freedom here, maybe put Rita and the kids around the back . . .

So I said, "I don't think . . ." and just bided my time, because I just didn't feel the vibes. Still, it seemed like a great accomplishment, and the Wailers started to buckle down. There were lots of rehearsals and much serious work—along with plenty of football (soccer) games.

Then Chris released the Wailers' first album, *Catch a Fire*. It was an instant hit, and that was it, the beginning of great things. The Wailers toured England and then the States, even opening for Sly and the Family Stone in Las Vegas. Back in Jamaica, everybody started wooing, wanting to meet them because they were now celebrities, signed with Island. It was even reported in the *Gleaner*, Jamaica's main newspaper, "The Wailers have now signed . . . etc., etc.," and so it was, *whew*—everybody be friends now. Big Time!

And I watched this and thought, o-*kay*. I was seeing a different sort of life coming in . . . and the girls. Soon, Chris had set up Esther Anderson at Hope Road; she was a former lover of his (I was later told), an actress born in Jamaica but living in London, who had just made a movie with Sidney Poitier. Her new assignment was to work as the Wailers' photographer and to do public relations for their upcoming tour. Others living there were Diane Jobson, who eventually became one of Bob's lawyers and was the sister of Chris's best friend and business partner Dickie Jobson (also a tenant), and Cindy Breakspeare, who later became involved with Bob. Diane and Cindy, like most of the women who hung out at Hope Road, were pretty, brown-skinned, uptown, middle-class characters, having a fling at doing their own thing. So to them Bob was *sooo* attractive and they were *soooo* attracted. They all wanted to go to bed with him, and he made himself available by starting to sleep there at night. But I don't want to put it entirely in a negative way, since this opportunity made it possible for him to create what he did. It was a real beginning, because so much that he had wanted for his music really started when he was given this house.

There was nonstop activity at 56 Hope Road. At any given time meetings, rehearsals, interviews were going on, and some people would be exercising on the floor. The kitchen ran twenty-four hours a day. Soups

would be cooking, or sometimes Bob or his friend Alan "Skill" Cole, a soccer star, would be standing there making peanut juice, this juice, that juice.
Hope Road was where Bob's life seemed to open up, and he started to feel
"Yeah!" And I was happy for him, coming as he did from the poverty of
St. Ann and Trench Town. I think our early life made us uneasy, that it
pained us to say we had had such rough times. I still think we had fun, and
that was important. Even in the shortness of Bob's life he was able to enjoy
some of it, to do the things that his spirit told him it wanted to do; he
couldn't fight that. And I think God loved him more for all the sacrifices he
made, not just for himself but so others could live so happily. I asked him
when he passed on to be at the right hand of the Almighty, so that when I
get there I'll see him. I'm looking forward to that.

Despite my misgivings, I showed up at Hope Road almost every day,
just to be a part of what was happening. If one night Bob didn't come
home, I'd be there the next morning asking why. And then there would
be the explanations, because there were always explanations. Most of the
time he'd say, "It's rehearsal." So it was the music keeping him, and I'd say,
"Well, I can't fight that because that's your dream and that's what we're
gonna eat bread from, so if it takes rehearsal to get things together . . . But
you just be careful!" As always, I was supportive of what Bob did and never
lost my confidence. I even bought him a bedroom set for Hope Road but he
didn't want it, he didn't want the place to feel like home, or to look too
much like he wasn't home!

By then he was supporting his family very well, and he was generous
with money, as he had always been even when he had only small amounts
to give. "Here, this is for you and Aunty and the children," he'd say. And I
was easy with him. I'd say, "Oh, nice," and not mention anything else that
might be on my mind, even though the Hope Road facility was getting to
be a thorn in our lives. Every time I'd see all the goings-on, I'd think, *uh, uh,*

I would never move into this, I would be depleted. It all seemed like a coop, and I would be the little black girl in the ring.

Most importantly, all this music was now going on without me. I wasn't singing with Bob or anyone else now. That was a big change in my life, but I had worked hard and needed some time out. Let me see what's up, I thought. Some of my friends warned me, "He's ready for big times now, Rita, watch dem gal deh." But I said, "No, I just have to wait and see, I'm not gonna be fallin' and dyin'." Sometimes Bob and I would quarrel about the situation, but in the end I decided that if that's what it takes to *be* somebody, go ahead. He kept saying I should come to Hope Road if I wanted to move from Aunty's, that the house was there, with a big yard, and they must find space for me and the children. At this point, though, I just wanted my independence. I wanted to leave Trench Town, yes, but not at the expense of my self-respect. As I've said, I always had myself in mind.

Still, I had trouble thinking I was going to "separate" from Bob, that I would be the one to leave the marriage. So I looked up Gabby, a Rastafarian elder, someone I respected and could ask advice of. He seemed to already have some knowledge of the Hope Road scene and was not too pleased by what he referred to as Bob's "diversion." I explained to Gabby that I didn't want to live there, that I wasn't going to become someone else—to "get out of myself" was the way I thought of it—just to please Bob. It'd be wrong, I told Gabby. I'd feel strange up in there with the children and everyone coming and going. And what privacy would we get, living in a place with a perpetually open gate, open to friends and all this and all that? I just couldn't stand for my kids to live so.

By then I had mentioned to Aunty that I was looking to take myself and the kids out of her house. "You better think about it!" she said in her usual way. "Nobody's gonna rent you a house with them four pickney! Don't even bother try!"

But Gabby seemed to understand and was very well there when I needed help. His only questions were, "But why you want to move from Trench Town?" and "Does Bob agree?"

And I had to say, "I've always wanted to leave Trench Town, and I don't care if Bob agrees. My children are growing bigger every day and the life they are growing up to see is not what I want it to be."

Soon after, Gabby called to say that there was a government housing scheme—with concrete block houses for sale—going up in Bull Bay, about twelve miles away, on the south coast. And that kind of threw me out. "Bull Bay!" I said. "It's so *far!*"

But Gabby happened to know about the project because he lived there, and he described it as pleasant and easy enough to get to. So I said yes, I'd love to look at it, and a few days later he came for me.

We drove along the coast and then into a small, quiet community, and I looked at the houses that were available. Gabby said I should choose the one I liked and then get the money from Bob. "Mek Bob go to the Minister of Housing and deal with it," he said. By now, because of his new celebrity, Bob had become friendly with people in high office, ministers of this and ministers of that. But I didn't feel like asking Bob directly, because I knew he wanted me to move to Hope Road.

His friend Alan Cole, though, was someone I found approachable. "Alan," I said casually, as soon as the opportunity arose, "I'm not waiting on Bob. You as his friend know I need to get a house to take my children to, now could you speak to the Minister of Housing for me?"

The Minister of Housing at that time was Anthony Spaulding, a good man, a *very* good man, who said, "Sure!" and managed it immediately— "Wife want a house, mek wife get a house!"

Bob remained skeptical about all this, but by then I had started to hear rumors about him and Esther Anderson, and I realized that things were going from bad to worse, that I just had to make up my mind and take my kids out of this mess. Chris Blackwell had connected Bob with Esther as part of the package—not only would she be his photographer, she would take him to England to promote the recordings. The record company was really forming a relationship to have the two of them as a public image. (Promoters do that.) From what I was seeing, though, it was private as well as public, and it was too close for comfort.

A couple of days later I got money from Bob, despite his initial disapproval, for the house I had chosen. The down payment was something like three thousand dollars for a two-bedroom house. Like Aunty's it was a basic structure, period—but it was concrete block, in a good area, and it was brand new. Before I signed for it, Minister Spaulding said I should go take another look, just to be sure. So he gave me the keys and the next morning I took three buses out to Bull Bay—not so easy to get to, as Gabby had thought.

My house—number 15 Windsor Lodge—was on a dirt road off the main road and then off a little drive onto a dead end with only one other house. It had no lights, no water, no gate, no nothing. The government builds you this little thing and it's *as is*—take it or leave it. But there were avocado and tamarind trees on the property, and you could smell the sea; in fact, I had seen a footpath off the main road that went right to the water. There wasn't a sound that morning except the birds in the trees. I felt so peaceful, standing there, and if the deal was take it or leave it, I couldn't leave it. So I went back to Mr. Spaulding's office in Kingston, handed over the money, and signed my name.

I took the keys home and said, "Aunty, I've gotten a house in Bull Bay," hoping she'd be as excited as I was, though predictably she wasn't. There she stood, all five feet of her, saying, "You're crazy! You shouldn't do that! You can't go without Robbie and where is Robbie and why Robbie don't help you?"

"Oh no, Aunty," I said, "Robbie's fine. He's into making his music and what have you."

She said, "You'll never manage a house. You need to let Robbie go where he's going, and you stay here and take care of the children."

I said, firmly but as gently as I could, "No, Aunty." Because I was beginning to understand how threatened she was by my leaving. In spite of her complaints, we were her life, and she needed us as we had always needed her.

She said, "But why are you going all that *way*?"

"So people won't trouble me and the children when Bob don't come home," I said. She had commented enough about that.

"You going all that way to Bull Bay, and how am I going to see the children?"

I said, "You'll see them."

She wouldn't give up, she just wasn't the type. She said no, she was not impressed, it was too far, and "We don't know anybody out there."

I didn't say anything. I just held the keys in my hand and waited until she left the room.

Next day I went looking for a truck and found an old wooden-body one that I wasn't sure would make it because it was so raggedy. But the guy was making a little money, and it was cheap. The trip had to be cheap or it couldn't happen. I stared at the truck for a while and then said, "Okay, that's great." The driver must have seen my concern, because he said, "Are you sure, Mrs. Marley?" Somehow, just his saying that convinced me. "Yes!" I said. "Let's do it!"

I got that truck on faith, because I had only a few dollars left after having made the down payment, and I hadn't seen Bob since then. But I convinced myself that the money would come somehow. Bob will have money, I told myself, I'll go past Hope Road and get some. Because I had to *move*. I had to get the kids out of that environment—mentally as well as physically. And it had to happen right away because if it didn't, they would be exposed to, and maybe drift into, another, looser lifestyle. It was kind of a shock to them that Daddy was now living that way and that they had to see Mommy not happy sometimes.

The following morning, early, the truck came down to the house. I hadn't told Aunty. Clearly, even at twenty-six years old and with four children, I was still very much under her thumb. When she saw the truck she said, "Really?" And when I nodded, she said, "You're crazy, you don't really mean this."

I finally had to speak straight out. I said, "You say I'm a big woman now, Aunty, even though I'm still young, but you shouldn't make me feel like I'm not able to make my own decisions. And I'm not being ungrateful for what you have done."

"And Robbie's not going?"

"No, he's not. And I'm not gonna ask him, either."

So I packed up and she watched me, and though she helped she was so sad. Finally I said, "Come with me then if you're going to feel that way!" But she had her house too and she couldn't just leave. Poor Aunty—but I had to be strong, because I didn't want to leave her feeling like that, even though she was hinting that I would never make it without her. So I said, "Aunty, don't worry, you know where we are, come tomorrow. But I'm going today."

She said, "But there's no light there."

I said, "No problem, we have candles, don't worry. But I want to go before it gets dark; it'll be easier to unload."

By this time it seemed as if everybody in the neighborhood had gathered at the truck and at the gate, and they were all saying, "Lord, they're going to Bull Bay to live," as if we were going to the moon. But I packed the kids in there and they were so excited and happy because to them this was fun. "We're moving! We're going to a different house and we will be driving there in this truck!" And I was just there absorbing the whole scene and thinking, oh my god, please make this work.

When we got to Hope Road, the first person we saw was Esther Anderson, leaning over the upstairs porch. I said, "Good morning, is Bob there? Can I see Bob?" I knew he was up there in the room with her.

"What do you want?" she said. "Why you come here?"

This gal is crazy, I thought. But I didn't want to get into it with her, especially in front of the children, so I just said again, "Is Bob there? Is Robbie there?"

"He's sleeping!" she said.

"Then please wake him up for me, it's important."

"Why don't you leave him alone?" she said. "Why you won't let the man sleep?"

And then I lost my cool. "Who do you think you're talking to?" I said, louder than I'd meant to.

"Why don't you stop breeding?" she shouted. "All you do is breed! Bob needs a career, and you need to stop breeding and let him find a life!"

I couldn't believe it! I just stood there and said, "Whew!" And then I thought, oh no no no, let's get out of here. But by then all the noise had woken Bob up anyway, and he came down and said to me, "What's happening? Why you down here trying to create a scene?"

"Me?!!" I yelled. "Don't you talk to me like that! You have that whore up there . . ." And I got really angry, because if she didn't respect me she should at least have respected the fact that I had my children with me, and that's my husband she's sleeping with! So I really whopped it to her, and I cursed him too. And after he gave me the money I asked for, I got back in the truck and told the driver to *drive!*

Bob said he would come by later, which I knew he would do, and also that he'd try to chat me up. But the last I said to him was, "F- - - you, Bob, I'm very disappointed in you!" I was so upset, because that was the first time I'd ever gotten into that woman thing. And I didn't intend to argue with her, because if I had any argument it was with him.

When he got there that night, he looked around and said, "How could you do this to me and the children? It's a mistake, Esther just takes pictures of the group, and Chris Blackwell put her there to live . . . until she goes back to London . . ."

When I didn't answer this, he said, "You're really serious? No light, no water, no nothing? You gonna stay out here with the kids? 'Cause I have to go to England to do promotion for this new album."

I said, "Yeah yeah yeah yeah, I'm staying."

I could see he liked coming out here, to the clean air. He looked at me, eye to eye. "You okay?" he said.

"I'm fine," I said. I didn't mention how angry I was, I let that pass because I didn't want to start anything in front of the kids, who were still up waiting for Daddy to come.

Then he looked at the four of them, who were obviously happy, gorging on the takeout fried chicken we'd stopped for. To them all this was a lark. "You okay?" he asked.

"We're fine!" they yelled. "We love Bull Bay!" A big, loud chorus.

Maybe he was surprised by their response. He seemed very subdued after that. I watched him leave, his head kind of bent, like it was heavy. I thought I should have a heavy heart to match, but instead I just felt sad but free, and very relieved.

And there was something about that night that I found so exciting! The children soon fell asleep, but I couldn't go to bed. I realized I was too happy! I kept walking around, out to the yard and then back inside, saying to myself, I have a house! A house!

I don't remember how late it was when I blew out the last candle still burning and stood in the doorway one more time. Everything I'd gone through that day—with Aunty, Bob, Esther Anderson—it all seemed to have happened not to me but to another person. In the silence I could hear the children breathing behind me and, faintly in the distance, the waves on the shore. All I could think of was that we were finally out of Trench Town, and that I was standing, almost unbelievably, in the doorway of a house of my *own*. I couldn't decide which of those two things pleased me the most.

Next morning Aunty was there by eight. She had taken the three buses! Poor Aunty. She said, "I couldn't sleep. I couldn't sleep. How could I sleep without the children? Without you? Look at them! Did you bathe them last night?"

I said, "Yes Aunty, they bathed, don't worry." Of course we hadn't bathed; by the time we'd arrived and unpacked it was full dark. But after Aunty came that day we went to the beach and bathed there, and the kids were ecstatic. And soon a friend brought barrels of water for us regularly, while my application to the minister for utilities went through. We were the first in the community to have electricity, and it pleased me that we weren't the last, that our presence there meant that neighbors had it too, because soon the area was full of people moving into the new government houses.

Eventually everyone got used to the idea of our being there, especially after I began to decorate the house, painting it red, green, and gold, and planting a garden. I was more content than I had been in so long, because I was helping myself, doing what I wanted to do. And, most important of all, I was independent, if not financially, then at least in terms of being on my own.

For a while I took life easy, going to the beach, jogging every morning, getting fresh fish to eat. I assumed, finally, some of the responsibilities Aunty had always held on to. I focused on the kids, on their schooling and all the other needs of growing children. I felt strong and proud of myself. And I started making demands on Bob. Instead of feeling sorry for him now, I was saying, "I need your help. I'm not doing housework in Jamaica. For anybody! I'm only going to do *certain* things here in Jamaica. You're taking the steps you have always wanted to, so remember we are here."

But as I've said, Bob was very giving, there was never a *mean* time. I never said "We need" or "I want " and didn't get. That's Bob, that's the way he always was. And then, if we'd had a quarrel, he would come and bring me flowers, fruit, or the chocolate I love. And I would be . . . "No no, man." Until things would start to get nice, and you nice, and . . . then I'd give in, and we'd make love, and then would come the promises.

Though Bob and I remained married for the rest of his life, Esther Anderson wasn't the first and wouldn't be the last woman he was involved with. I guess the way I saw it was that he was not the man for their lives, but their man for a time. I never made friends with any of them; I didn't have to. Their relationships with Bob were "off the record," and he kept them away from me for the most part, or I was careful, usually, not to go anywhere I'd meet them. I didn't see myself chasing after him. I tried to train myself to think of Bob as a good loving brother more so than a real husband, and made my peace with the situation. I asked God for help with the things I couldn't change. Maybe because there were so many women they grew less and less threatening, even though some had children—the boys born while I was in Delaware were not the last born outside our marriage, and I ended up taking care of many of them.

The early seventies was a very different time, too. It all had to be for a reason, I thought. Bob remained a loving father and friend. I still respect that, still give him respect on that. Sometimes it hurt—*ah*, I can't deny it. But then I'd tell myself, *uh-uh*, that's not the eye for you to look through. Look through another eye. Rastafari.

chapter eight
I KNOW A PLACE

BEFORE THE GOVERNMENT stepped in to build the housing scheme at Bull Bay, it had been a very bad gang area. People were afraid to pass there, afraid they'd be blown away. At the end of 1972, when we arrived, the neighborhood was peaceful but the look of the place was just beginning to change. Like Trench Town, most of its houses had been built from anything available on any land that seemed available, and you didn't see too many concrete government houses like mine. All around was bush—just bush, a few farms, the beautiful blue water, and the beach (which I love).

As soon as we got settled, I enrolled Sharon, Cedella, and Ziggy at Bull Bay All Age Elementary. Stephen was still a toddler. After school they had the Windsor Lodge Community Center, with a park where they could play football with the other children in the neighborhood. Every once in a while, walking them to school in the morning, I felt as if I were dreaming. And although I had sad moments as well as happy ones, I still feel that this is where my life, my own independent life, started.

But I realized I couldn't be *fully* independent until I learned to drive.

I had been trying—maybe I should say I'd been dreaming of driving, but it wasn't until I got to Bull Bay that driving became a real necessity. I wasn't going to pay three bus fares to get to and from Kingston! Time you have to wait on the bus to get home, which took two hours, and then to cook dinner for the kids, oh . . . no way. So I got busy on that immediately.

Back when we were still in Trench Town, we'd had one of those big sixties station wagons that Bob got for very cheap. I was eager to learn to drive but, like many husbands I hear about, he wasn't patient enough to teach me, so I took driving lessons when we could afford them, which wasn't often. One day Bob parked the station wagon at the gate and I decided that I was going to show him that I could drive. I got in, put the emergency down, got the car into gear, and drove down to the bottom of the road. When it was time to turn around, though, I wasn't able to find reverse. People gathered around, watching me fight with the gear stick and making suggestions. I sent someone to call Bob, and *he* sent someone to say he wasn't coming, I should find a way to come back. Eventually a guy we knew named Reggie, a guitarist with the Upsetters, arrived and said he'd find reverse for me, which he did, and then drove me back up to the house. I decided after that episode that I wasn't going to be embarrassed again.

When we moved to Bull Bay, Reggie began coming out to give me lessons. Afterward, he'd take me into Kingston to do my errands or up to Hope Road. One day he was driving me, in the little Morris Minor we had then, and he wasn't paying attention to the road and almost hit someone. I got angry, and said, "Why don't you drive properly? Look where you're going, man!!!"

I suppose he didn't like my attitude, because he said, "Why don't you drive yourself?!!!"

I said, "One day I will! You'll see!"

We could have left it at that, but I guess he wanted a fight, because he said, "If you don't like my driving, why don't you let Bob drive you?"

"Don't call my husband's name into this!!" I shouted.

But Reggie wouldn't quit. "Why don't you let Bob teach you to drive?" he said.

That was it for me! I said, "Get out of my car!" And I boxed him, *bow!*

He jumped out of the car, and I imagine he was thinking, oh yes, let's see how far she thinks she can drive.

But I got behind that steering wheel and left him standing in the road and drove myself slowly into Kingston. And it was funny to see the look on Bob's face as he watched me navigate the circular driveway at Hope Road. He seemed happy but was so surprised all he could say was, "Hey, you're driving!" Then he realized who was missing and said, "But what did you do with Reggie?"

After that I got a license, everything that was necessary. And oh, I felt as if I'd taken another step forward. Still, I hardly ever felt like going anywhere far. I rarely went out, except to shop or to show up at Hope Road or take the kids for a drive. Then one day I discovered lice in Ziggy's hair—he'd caught them from someone in the local school. So I took all the kids out of there and enrolled them elsewhere, which meant I had to drive them to school every morning.

For me this was a learning time. Bob was still coming and going when he felt like, which was cool with me. I was learning to live not only by myself with the kids, but without a full-time man—and not so much physically as emotionally. I even realized that, ah, well, I might even have to take up a divorce one day soon, considering how we were now living. It felt so strange to me, sometimes I found myself wondering, "What kind of arrangement is this?" I had to keep reminding myself that I'd been told that part of the situation came with success, and that this success had provided our house and other advantages—the food we ate, for one very important thing (I never forgot to give thanks that we'd stopped being hungry). And then there were the rooms I was planning to add to the main structure, and the garden . . . I had to be more patient, I decided, and better able to cope in order to maintain my mentality, so that whatever else was happening wouldn't drive me crazy. I couldn't do that, I had to keep a cool head so that I could raise my family. They were my focus now. And on good days, thinking about Bob, I'd say to myself, oh, let all those women turn him on, I'm just gonna love my children, love myself, and see what comes out of it.

And—I guess this is most important—I still felt like Rita. I never gave up on me fully, never forgot me and absorbed everything. I was always able to reserve Rita, because this is how I'd started out, being called "blackie tootus" and being forced to say I'm gonna *be* somebody. So I was not giving anyone the privilege to totally destroy Rita. Rita meant something, Rita came for a purpose. Rita had a life to live.

There was a period soon after I moved to Bull Bay when Bob stayed away for almost two full months and we didn't know where he was. I heard he was in England, I heard he was in Negril. During that time Esther Anderson was touring with the Wailers, but that may have been the end of their relationship. (A couple of years ago she came to Jamaica to say she and Bob had built a house in Negril. With her money, she said. I don't know if she thought I was going to claim it now, but I want nothing to do with it!) But back then she was with Bob for a while, and we couldn't find him, until one day he turned up at the house in Bull Bay.

I was surprised and definitely unprepared when I heard his car coming up the road. I went out to the yard and there he was. I couldn't even think of anything to say so I just said, "Where were you?"

And he said, "I don't know!"

I'd been alone with the kids much of the time when Bob went off into his "I don't know" program. There were many lonely days and nights. Of course, Aunty came regularly if I needed to go somewhere and couldn't take Stephen, and sometimes she'd stay overnight if it got late. Friends helped out with the heavy stuff, like bringing water from the main community pipe.

I needed a lot of water, because I was determined to plant a garden. The soil in the yard was poor, largely sandy soil from the seabed. People told me, "Ah you're crazy, you can't plant there." But I said, "Wait, I'm gonna show you." And the expression on their faces when they saw my collards, my spinach, my papayas!

In later years, when I was touring, I'd bring all kinds of things home. Each time I'd go somewhere I couldn't wait to return because I'd be carrying this or that to my home to do this, do that. It had room for improvement! I built a veranda, and a wall around the property, and planted a lawn for the kids, where they'd play gunfight, or dollhouse, or school (with Sharon as teacher), or something that involved tree climbing—it seemed as if they were always *doing* something. And Aunty would teach them songs just as she had taught me. Just to see them thriving in the clear air and space—at last out of that one little room in Trench Town—was enough to convince me that coming to Bull Bay had been the right move. I still give thanks to Gabby for it.

Windsor Lodge was real homey, and I think of it that way even now, I guess because it was my first home and has a lot of sentiment to it. Which is why I can't give it up—recently I called my lawyer to ask, "Where is the title to Windsor Lodge?" He called me back and said, "It's here, Mrs. Marley, you have the title, you still own that property." It's such a *nice* place and sometimes I think I should refurbish it—even the mango tree is still there and bearing. In any case, I can't let it go. My kids are fond of it too; it holds a lot of memories for all of us. After they grew up and started to earn money, Ziggy and Steve built an adjoining place on the property where they still come to relax. "Oh Mommy," they tell me, "out there it's so nice, that's where we go when we want to meditate on something." So when people say to me, why don't you just sell it, get rid of it, you don't *need* it, I say no, no, no. This was my beginning—how could you want to sell your beginning?

· · ·

When Bob wasn't on the road he'd come out to Bull Bay to see the kids, even though our own relationship was almost at the point where I'd become just "Rita the friend" or "Rita the sister." Sometimes he'd bring other women, like the American Yvette Anderson, whom he wanted me to help with some publishing thing. A lot of our friends shrugged off his behavior, saying "This is what happens." Others just couldn't understand why it was happening and really disapproved. But the fact that other people sympathized with me didn't change how I decided to deal with it—which was that I saw it and wasn't going to fight it. Because, despite everything— all the rumors as well as what I could see with my own eyes—most of the women still came with an explanation: "This one is happening because she does my pictures," or "Island sent her to do this or that," or "Yvette Anderson is here because she's an American, she can have my publishing work done properly." So there was always a reason for each of them— especially when they came to Jamaica to stay with him at Hope Road while the children and I were living in Bull Bay, in what we spoke of as "the family house."

After the two-month Esther Anderson program, he never stayed away too long. Sometimes, especially when he'd come back from a tour, he'd come alone, or he would bring some of his friends, telling them, "Come let me show you *my* house!" Because that was still "coming home" for him. Often his line was that nothing was happening at Hope Road, "them just living and having fun, plenty rehearsal and music business so/so," but "nobody thinking about planting," and "oh, you come to this garden, man, you don't want to leave!"

And because there were times that he really *didn't* want to leave, I had a basement room dug behind the kitchen, which we used as a studio. We put in a little tape recorder, and when it got hot he would come and sit down there. Because to us it would not be a life without music. At night after the kids had gone to bed and we'd finished cleaning up the kitchen, after all was quiet, we'd go down there—sometimes to make out, of course, because that was our little nest—but more often just to rehearse and compose. And it was a daytime thing too—we spent pretty nice Sundays right there with the kids. The house was always full, because I usually had other children coming for care and attention. Neighborhood kids would drop by—"Mrs. Marley home?"—as well as Bob's friends. But this was our domain. In some small way having it kept me more involved in the music, in what I loved.

Bob had a little Capri then, and if the kids were out in the yard playing and heard the car coming and recognized its distinctive sound, they'd start yelling, "Daddy's coming, Daddy's coming!" Because whatever was going on between the two of us, he always loved his kids and paid as much attention to them as he could—running around the house in a Frankenstein mask and trying to scare everyone, Cedella remembers. Even today she says he was the softy and I was the disciplinarian—that when he saw any of the children upset, "we knew we were going to the ice-cream parlor!" And he was very ambitious for all of them, always willing to provide school fees or uniform money and advising them to continue their education. Occasionally he took them to school himself, which was a big deal for them—"That's my Daddy!"

But music was our food. It had always been our entertainment, our pleasure. And when you find out early enough that your kids are extraordinarily talented and are following in your footsteps, there is certainly no way you're *not* going to encourage them. So we had our little "events" in the cellar. We'd say, "Okay, this is the Marley Show! Audition time now! Come do what you can!" We trained them, not professionally or purposely, but because this is how I remembered learning how to sing, the way Dream and I had always amused ourselves, learning songs and harmony from Papa and Aunty and Uncle Cleveland back in Trench Town. And now we had our little audition area—where "Tomorrow we're going to have concert now! Showtime!" Everybody would start getting their little thing together, their act—"And this is what I'm gonna do for Mommy, and this is what I'm gonna do for Daddy!" It was fun, fun, fun!

· · ·

With Bob so often absent, daily life was more difficult, although I didn't lack friends who would check on us. Besides Gabby, who had been so helpful in finding the house for me and was now my neighbor in Bull Bay, I had another good friend, Owen Stewart, a Jamaican soccer star known familiarly as Tacky.

Because he knew I was married, Tacky wasn't into our friendship for sex or having a girlfriend (although eventually we did develop a relationship). But he was one of those who felt sympathetic toward me because of the way Bob was treating me. In fact, he had occasion to witness the different women Bob sometimes brought to the house, and he was there to ask why. As for Bob, even before Tacky and I became involved, when he just *thought* we had a relationship, he became irrationally possessive.

Once he saw Tacky with me and wanted to fight! He had just come back from one of his tours, and I guess his friends told him that Rita could be very close with Tacky. He came by the house one morning and the kids told him that Tacky and I had gone to the river for water—the government took its time about laying the pipes. When Bob showed up there (as usual with a girl in the car), he left the girl and came down to the riverbank, yelling, "Hey, Tacky, you're seeing my woman! And blah blah blah . . ." And carried on like a wild man!

But Tacky said, "No Bob, we can't fight, we're brethren. And I'm here because she needs help. She needs someone, and you must respect that." Tacky went very hard on him. And Bob was sorry for the accusation and did admit it. Poor Bob. He could always see the truth and he knew nothing was going on then between Tacky and me.

But I got very upset. I said to Bob, "After all you're doing, you're going to accuse *me?* What about that bitch you have in the car?"

The next time he went off to London, just about 1973, it was quite obvious that he'd started having women right in my face. At one point I thought there must have been something personal going on between him and Diane Jobson, but I guess she lived to overcome it when she became his lawyer. When I'd ask him, though, it was always the same story: Everyone came for a purpose. "This one's for this, so don't get upset, and this one's for that." But it had become too obvious. I felt that I was being taken for a ride, and it seemed like it was going to be a *long* ride. So I decided I wasn't going to play the game. I told him plain, straight out, if you're going to be doing this, we will not have a sexual relationship. We will have a relationship because we're already family, but as far as sexual involvement is concerned, no. We didn't have AIDS at that time, but there were other diseases, and I refused to be exposed to that kind of thing.

By then Tacky was already coming by sometimes to keep me company. He was my *good* friend, I knew I could always call on him when I needed help. Although at first it had been strictly a friendship situation—"I see you're here with the children, and I don't see Bob coming around"—now there were evenings when I got lonely and wanted to see someone. Because living in that location for the first time, anything could have happened to us, and we needed—*I* needed—someone. Not living in, because I've never done that, but just around me when Bob didn't come home for a couple of weeks. Tacky would come in the morning to see how is everything, was everything all right last night, you had no problem? Often he'd bring fish, or Irish moss, all the "ital" stuff—foods that Rastafarians eat. Tacky is a very handsome Rastaman, who looks a lot like Bob. He was very respectful of the family, and caring; sometimes he'd even take the kids to school or take me to town in his yellow van. He had a job as an accountant in a big office in Kingston, and I found him intelligent and a reasonable man. We had a lot in common, so eventually I found myself attracted to him as well as grateful for his attention, and we developed a relationship that I thought was normal.

The next time Bob came back to Jamaica, I was almost raped. Because this is where I had drawn the line—"I'm not having sex with you." But he insisted: "You're my wife and I want you!" And so we had sex, and I think that's when I got pregnant again. When I discovered I was going to have another child, my first thought was, my God, what is this—because, despite trying to overlook everything and be the good sister, I was so sick of his ways! (By then he had another outside baby, a daughter born in London.) But he knew that Tacky and I had a relationship; he and Tacky had a meeting—he sent for Tacky to discuss the matter. But during the meeting in came Bob's current girlfriend, Cindy Breakspeare, saying, "Oh darling . . ." And Tacky said, "Look at that, Bob." So Tacky brought him down again, and Bob felt bad about that too, because he would rather she had not appeared at a time when he was trying to correct something that he was so wrong about!

After that, at least for a while, it seemed as if we weren't going to be intimate anymore. Still, he just couldn't bear to know that I might find somebody who loved me as a woman. And I wasn't trying to prove that I could; it just so happened that someone was there for me, and that really saved me. Because the frustration and the insult that I had to face with Bob's lifestyle was, in spite of the good face I showed to the world, killing me. It could have killed me. So I think God sent me a friend when I needed one.

Still, I had promised myself I wasn't going to be falling and dying, and this meant that I had to keep an eye on what was happening at Hope Road. Some of Bob's girlfriends were upset because I was always there, seeing everything. I heard that one of them said, "Oh, she's getting serious here!" And that's exactly what was happening. I *was* getting serious.

From the first, when the whole thing started there, I'd felt a little bit outside of it. I don't know if it was again the color of my skin or my Rasta philosophy that caused me to feel that way. The uptowns came to Island House out of curiosity, since it was in their territory, although Bob Marley and the Wailers were new to them; while our friends from the ghetto knew the music scene they were coming into if not much about the neighborhood where it had relocated. So the population at the house was a mixture. That part was okay. Additionally, I felt outside because of my personal feeling. So it took a while for me to figure out how I should be a part and yet not be a part.

My third daughter, Stephanie, was born in 1974, and in an effort to feed our large family healthy foods, grown organically according to Rastafarian precepts, and because I'd had such success with my home garden, I'd gone into full-time farming. St. Ann was too far away from Kingston, but a farm in Clarendon Parish, which is much closer, had been up for sale. So Bob bought it for us, and then I started to reap things like coconuts (and more coconuts!), naseberries, star apples, oranges, almost everything that you would think of coming off a farm, all of it organically grown. Recently I gave a portion of the land to the Rastafarian movement; the Nyabinghi Brothers built a tabernacle where they worship, and there's a section of it that they farm; they also have accommodations for women and children, and a school.

But back then I would be collecting all this produce, which turned out to be far too much for one family, and I thought, what am I gonna do with it? I gave away a lot to friends, but there was still a surplus—we even had goats and cows! Then it occurred to me to ask Bob to let me open a little "depot" at Hope Road. Every day there were rehearsals there, or meetings or some such; the place was always crowded, a packed house of musicians and fans. The scene was like a party, with a lot of hungry and thirsty people who had nowhere to go for refreshment. So I thought I might do something different, and one morning I said to Bob, "You know, I think I could do a juice bar over there, right beside the gate."

He frowned a bit, then laughed and said, "You sure? What would you do?"

I said, "Sell things, and so forth." I realized the word "things" wasn't specific, but I meant it, because if one thing didn't work, I was going to try something else. And if I had to sell oranges, they would be the best oranges in Jamaica! So I explained that I could sell coconuts (in their shell, with a straw) and I could make juices with the different fruits that we were getting. And so he agreed, because he believed in my abilities—he'd sometimes say, "Whatever Rita says always works."

We hadn't thought about doing food before I started this, since we didn't think we'd be allowed to in a residential area. But the idea of selling things was already in place: By then we sold records and anything else having to do with music. And I had a history of "selling things" successfully. So Bob said, only a little bit doubtfully, "That's not a bad idea, if that's what you want to do."

I said, "Yeah, let me try." I just wanted something to occupy my time, in terms of not sitting down and waiting, or not having anything to do but stay home and do housework. My babies were fine, they were growing up with us, and it was fun to have—if not a career—then at least something else to do that I enjoyed. So I created the Queen of Sheba Restaurant, and when I began to bring the food everybody went crazy. They loved it! Even my avocados were different—when it was avocado time, I had the best. And coconuts, oranges, star apples . . . When it comes to growing, I know I'm really God blessed, because whatever I plant grows. Whenever my fruit trees are bearing, they bear exceptionally well—big and good—and organic, because I don't ever, *ever* use any fertilizer other than manure. After the juice bar took off, I built a brick oven to bake whole wheat bread right there. Bob was my best customer. I still thought I should be around my husband to be sure he ate properly, and this was a way of doing it.

Not long after *Catch a Fire* made Bob Marley and the Wailers instant superstars, I remet my old friend Minnie Phillips, the Rasta sister from uptown Kingston who used to buy records from our little bedroom shop in Trench Town. One night Bob and I were at a gathering of a Rastafarian

A significant day in black history—February 11, 1966. Both of us wearing the same size smile!

Aunty Vie and my brother Wes—my caretakers.

The Wailing Wailers—Bunny, Bob, and Peter, 1966.

Bob's first recording, "One Cup of Coffee," 1973.

CHUCK KRALL/MICHAEL OCHS ARCHIVES.COM

Bob getting his usual hug
onstage with the I-Three,
Starlight Theater,
California, 1978.

MICHEL DELSOL

Me in one of my moods.

The Wailers—good to go at the Birmingham Odeon, 1974.

Rastaman vibrations—positive! Hammersmith Odeon in London, 1976.

"Could You Be Loved," Roxy Theater, Los Angeles, California, 1976.

The I-Three doing their thing. Starlight Theater, California, 1978.

Emperor of Ethiopia Haile Selassie I, King of Kings, Lord of Lords, Conquering Lion of the Tribe of Judah, Elect of God, at his coronation, November 2, 1930.

In the ghetto, bitter was sweet.

Studio One—Jamaica's Motown, where we started.

Our children, 1982.

Bob after performing in Madison Square Garden with the Commodores,
September 2, 1980.

A sad moment. With Steven and Ziggy at the state
funeral for Bob in Kingston, May 21, 1981.

Me in Central Park, doing one of my charity performances.

Picking up after him! At the Hollywood Walk of Fame
Awards Ceremony honoring Bob, with the Honorary
Mayor of Hollywood Johnny Grant. Los Angeles, 2001.

The Melody Makers got the gold for "Hey World"!

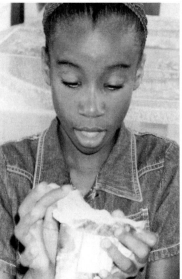

Serita (Washbelly), 1998.

With Stephanie at my usual birthday party in Ghana.

With Erykah Badu at James Bond Beach, Jamaica,
for a multi-artist tribute to Bob, 1999.

organization called the Twelve Tribes of Israel, and there was Minnie with Judy Mowatt, one of the top women reggae singers. I hadn't seen Minnie for eight or nine years, and as she says now, that night it was as if only the two of us were there. For hours we talked about old times and our children (like me, Minnie had had a few—Mike, Sahi, Saleh, Rutibel—in the years we'd been apart).

Before the night ended, we had planned a woman's organization, to be called Mada Wa Dada (Mother of the Nation). We knew it was going to take some money. One of our immediate goals was to build a school for Rasta children, since at that time in Jamaica a child who wore dreadlocks was not admitted into the government schools. (Some schools even now deny such children admittance.) Back then we thought we should take up that responsibility, we felt we had it on our shoulders. To raise money, we decided to put on a concert. Since we had the talent, and the promoters were using us to pack their houses, why couldn't we do it for ourselves? So we went to Bob—"Brother Bob, have mercy on the Rasta child!"—and he agreed to perform without pay. We were ecstatic, because that alone could fill the National Arena. Minnie was a Twelve Tribe member at the time, as was Bob, but I was not. Even though it was a Rasta organization, I didn't feel as if I had a part there, since I thought of it as a "mixing pot" and didn't see myself "mixing." Minnie was rebuked by the leaders of the organization for joining with me, a nonmember, to put this show together—it was "against the rules." (Their attitude toward women then needed adjustment, as women were always put in the background, which is why a women's organization was needed.) And they were the culprits in the long run, because Minnie trusted these brethren and had them at the gate controlling all the money, and they robbed us of every cent. Every last cent! The night after the concert we got nothing. Despite the fact that the National Arena had been packed and all the food sold off, we got nothing!

But after that Minnie hung with me, and a more loyal sister you could not find. Most important, she helped me create the Queen of Sheba

Restaurant. She'd be hook and hook with me, sometimes twenty-four seven. We would go to the Clarendon farm together and bring in the produce, set up the coconuts and the oranges. And Bob was so proud of us. He was like an agent pulling in customers, my proud PR man. He would tell everybody, "Go look over Rita's shop! Go get something over Rita's shop!"

Now I had a reason whenever I wanted to get away—I had to be off to the farm. If Bob was around, pretty soon I'd hear his Jeep coming in, and he'd be yelling, "Yo, Rita! Where are you?"

And I'd yell back, from between the rows of corn or coconut trees, "I'm over here, baby!"

He would sometimes be suspicious of me, and if he couldn't find me, he'd go up to Minnie's, looking, "Where's Rita???" And I might be somewhere sitting quietly, reading a book. I think it was his conscience, and as the song says, "In every man chest there beats a heart." I may have been resentful of this scrutiny then, but now I feel that he somehow had me in mind. That with all that was happening around him, innocent or not, he felt that some of it was not too good for Rita.

chapter nine
EASY SAILING

Something was still missing. I had a house, a farm, a shop at Hope Road, but I woke up most days with this: Suppose Bob and I should separate, what would I do? I felt I had to confront my dependency on someone who was so much in demand by the world. So I'd think, where do you really hang *your* hat? Are you gonna be wife? Or are you gonna be Rita? And who's Rita?

Because I knew I had the opportunity for a career and wanted more to do, I joined a drama group. Actually, it was more like a light opera troupe, a group of men and women who put on concerts every year. They had advertised in the newspaper for singers to audition, and after I was chosen I mentioned to Bob that I had a part in the upcoming concert. He was interested—not surprising, as he usually encouraged me in anything I tried to do. The singing was good for me, since I hadn't performed at all after moving to Delaware, and it felt good to use my voice, and to be onstage again, physically. I felt comfortable. But although I had fun, I knew I needed more of a challenge.

After coming home from Delaware I'd met up again with Marcia Griffiths, like Judy Mowatt one of Jamaica's top female singers. I'd known Marcia since the early days, when like me she was a Coxsone artist, young and pretty and skinny with a big voice. So we were aware of each other's potential. Since then her "Electric Boogie" had been a hit record in the States (and the source of the ever-popular Electric Slide), and she'd had another hit with Bob Andy in "Young, Gifted and Black." Marcia and I were already touching bases, listening to each other, when one day she called me to say that she was performing at the House of Chen in Kingston, one of Jamaica's well-known clubs at the time, and was wondering if I'd come along with Judy. "It would be good," Marcia said, "if both of you come in and let us just vibe together, just a little thing." She had already called Judy, who'd said, sure. So now it was up to me.

My first thought was, oh my god, as if I wasn't ready. But then I thought, *uh-uh*, being professionals as we were, it wouldn't be an assignment we needed time for. It wasn't as if I should say, "Oh no, we'd have to rehearse." So I told Marcia I'd call Judy and get it straight.

I had been seeing Judy, too. I'd first heard of her back in the sixties as the leader of a girl group, the Gaylettes, who were the top rivals to the Soulettes. We competed on the radio, although the Soulettes had an edge because we sometimes sang with the Wailers. Bob's friend Alan Cole was dating Judy back then, and he'd begun telling her about Rastafari. Judy was a good-looking young woman and into being glamorous, lots of bangles on her arm and all. But Alan would use me as an example, he was always going on about how Rita looked, and what Rita wore and didn't wear, saying, "Look at Rita! She's a big singer too, and you don't need all this hair style stuff." At the time, Judy had said, *"Uuff!"* I don't think she was ready to give up her bangles and her earrings to be a Rasta! But she did eventually. Like many of my friends, I had lost contact with her when I went to Delaware, but now I had remet her through Alan. I reached Judy that afternoon and we agreed it might be fun to "do a little thing" with Marcia.

I had to ask Aunty to come out to Bull Bay and babysit for me overnight, which I'd been trying not to do, in order to spare her, as she was now in her sixties—though she was as spry as ever. I picked up Judy and we went to the club and sat there watching Marcia onstage until, in the middle of her performance, she announced, "Ladies and Gentlemen, I have two of my best friends and sisters here with me tonight, Rita Marley and Judy Mowatt." And the place went crazy! We went up on the stage and sang "That's How Strong My Love Is"—no rehearsal, no nothing, just us. And we tore the place down! We had to encore continuously; the audience would not stop calling for more! And from there after we knew that, wow, we could do a thing, you know! And if you are not doing *your* thing, we could all come together and do *our* thing!

Lee "Scratch" Perry, after his failed attempt at performing, had become a producer. It was he who first billed the Wailers as "Bob Marley and the Wailers." When Chris Blackwell came into the picture, he continued to headline Bob, causing more than a little friction and confusion with the two other members, who felt as if they were losing Bob to the high-powered, high-living world of international music promotion. After their first successful tour, Bunny announced he would never again get on a plane. Peter was cooperative, though reluctantly, and never let his fury at Bob become evident. When their three-album contract with Island was finished, both Bunny and Peter decided they didn't want to have anything else to do with Blackwell, with touring and promoting concerts. It was arranged among them who would get this or that, and who would continue to get what. This was when Bob settled with Chris for the Hope Road property instead of money. Unlike the other Wailers, Bob re-signed with Island, as Bob Marley and the Wailers, but with new people as the Wailers.

Some people took the matter very deeply. I think the breakup of the group was more stressful to Bob than to either of the other two. He took it very very hard. He felt hurt and abandoned, and he never stopped thinking about it; that sadness was always a part of him. They'd been so young when they got together as the Wailers, and it was like being deserted by your brothers, especially in Bunny's case, since they were related through their sister Pearl. A lot of people still don't understand that this was such a hurt in Bob's life, that he took it with him. Because even when he was sick and losing gravity with life, he was saying they couldn't even call him. They never called him to say, "Bob, I love you." Peter was trying, I heard, on-stage, and Bunny also, but then it was too late, when they reached out.

The Island deal finished, everybody went out on their own. They each set up their own act—Peter started his company Intel Diplomat, Bunny had his Solomonic. And Bob achieved what he achieved and they achieved what they achieved. I'm a witness to the fact that Bob worked very hard, on the road and in the studio day and night; he was very serious about his work and the future welfare of his family. His achievement, which lives on, is testimony to that. And it's not about money, because he didn't begin to earn money until he went to rest. Money that he had he was using to build his own thing. He had to buy studio gear, he bought equipment for the band (he had hired his own band), and he was starting to own his career.

One morning, not long after Bunny and Peter's decision, I was in my garden at Bull Bay hanging the wash and watching Stephanie crawl around when Bob's driver came up the road, parked, jumped out of the car, and said, "Robbie said you should come down to the studio right away." When I asked, he insisted that nothing was *wrong*.

"Well," I said, "I can't just *leave* like this without any warning. What is it?"

He didn't know, he said, only that "Robbie just said it was an emergency."

It took a while for me to find the neighbor lady to look after Stephanie and change my clothes and everything, but I finally got it all together and drove to Hope Road, where they sent me to Harry J.'s studio in Kingston for a session.

Bob was there with some of his band members, and without revealing much he asked, "Where are your friends? Can you get your friends?"

I said, "What friends?"

"Marcia and Judy," he said.

Someone might have told him about our performance at the House of Chen, but he hadn't been there and if I had even mentioned it, I hadn't talked about it much. But it turned out that with Peter and Bunny gone, he was going to need backing support for work that he was doing. There was still some mystery surrounding this "emergency," but I said I would try to call Marcia and Judy, which I did, and they responded just as I had, as soon as they could. We went into the studio that afternoon and were told that we were supposed to be singing on a song called "Natty Dread." Of course, Bob knew of our separate abilities, whether or not he had heard about the three of us bringing down the House of Chen. But the fact remains that he hadn't heard us together until he heard us in the studio that day.

One thing about Mr. Marley: When you work for him, he pays you. And this was one of the respects that I always gave to him. When I was asked how much I was going to charge for this studio work on "Natty Dread," I looked at him and he looked at me quite businesslike—as if to tell me "Say it!"—and we laughed.

So I said, "Well, whatever you're giving Judy and Marcia, the same applies to me—and thank you!"

And he said, "No problem!" And flashed that sweet smile he had (when he wanted to use it).

Everybody loved what came out of the studio session that afternoon. And then it was finally explained that Bob had an album to deliver to Island, and now the big question was: Would we three sisters work with him? Would we go on a tour, finish the album, and work on the promotion?

After all those years with the Wailers and the Soulettes, and then the JAD thing, and singing and writing together on our own time in the little cellar studio, it was hardly new to me to work with him. But what really struck me now is that I would be paid. And I can't dismiss the sentimental part: Being able to be with him on the road meant so much to me, because we had decided to be friends again. There was no denying the fact that we still loved each other, and so were again living as man and wife, and I had just about started to be the *nagging* wife: "Where you going again?" "Why you have to go?"

I knew, at that point, that whatever I chose to do, I needed to pick myself up soon and do *something*. "Finding Rita" meant just that—making something happen. Marcia and Judy already had established solo careers, but they were eager to work steadily. So I looked at the two of them after Bob asked the question, and simultaneously—in harmony!—we all three yelled, "Yeah!"

It was one thing to be enthusiastic in the studio, and to be planning rehearsals and all that. But then I drove home and picked up Stephanie, and got the big kids from the Bull Bay Community Center, and didn't tell anyone anything about it, as I was still mulling over what would happen, how it could all be arranged.

Then, just as it was getting dark, Bob arrived. After the kids had climbed all over him, he pulled me down into the studio and said, oh so seriously, "You really want to come with me, Rita?"

And I said, "Well, why not?"

And he said, "Well, at least you'd be with me. We'd see each other every day."

And I thought that was great. He wanted me to be with him, if he was really going to go that way, as a solo performer with his own band and backup group. So we decided that we could do it, although that night we didn't expect such a tremendous reaction from audiences all over the world, or that we would tour together for seven years. And I never imagined that this would be the beginning of a long career for the I-Three, the group that Marcia and Judy and I formed.

Right then, Bob and I had only the moment in mind and were happy with the positive vibe. Nothing ventured, nothing gained, right? We figured that, hey, this is too good to stop, that even without Bunny and Peter, there was a way to go on. As the saying goes, one monkey don't stop the whole show. And this new way, which was after all a lot like the old way, seemed like a good way for everyone.

The first tour began in 1974, when Stephanie was still a baby. Again, it was Aunty to the rescue, because once more I had to leave the children with her. In order to accommodate us, she moved to Bull Bay, where she leased a piece of land from a little old man and built a house for herself. I suppose I needn't have worried about her being sixtysomething years old, because she was still so active. Truly an amazing lady. Aunty had two handhelpers this time, but she still built her own house. It was within walking distance of Windsor Lodge, so she would come down to the family house in the morning to run the show. A helper stayed with the children overnight, usually Miss Collins, an older lady who was Aunty's buddy. The children loved Miss Collins, who ended up living with us a long time as the family nanny.

That first tour was an experience—not just for me but for all of us—because this was big, and being sponsored by Island Records, and our group included a large entourage of press and photographers. It was also Bob's big break, the moment he had waited for. Our billing was still "Bob Marley and the Wailers" but consisted of different personnel—I think the I-Three were then included as Wailers, so this was exciting, too. Bob used to say that anyone who worked with him was a Wailer.

As much as the tour was an experience, it was also very much a trial run. Maybe not so much for Bob, who was ready, but certainly for the rest of us, because our earlier little concerts here and there had never exposed us to these kinds of crowds. People *came out* to see Bob Marley and the Wailers. The tour was well put together—we had our own bus and our own hotel rooms. At first I worried that I was going to be squished in with Bob and have to stay up all night, until I got it straight with the tour manager: "*No no no!* Out here I must be treated like an I-Three and not Mrs. Marley!" Even though I had to do the things that a wife would do, like make sure you get the wet clothes from the last performance, make sure you get the clothes out for the next concert, make sure to ask "Have you eaten? Did you eat?" And make sure—"It's bedtime!" Things like that—I still had to be that kind of a person on the road. But afterward I was privileged to be alone. I had my own room, I had my freedom, I could go shopping! I could do the things I wanted to do like a normal background vocalist! At the end of the day I was Rita!

So that was a wonderful experience for me, one that I really enjoyed. Naturally, there were certain things I missed. I hadn't realized how hard it might be to be away from the children. I was so attached to them now, from spending so much time with them and having had the leisure to have real conversations with them, and I missed them badly. Still, I knew Aunty was there for them, as she had been for me. A phone call a day kept my worries at bay, and Bob's too. At our sound check each day, first thing he'd say to me was, "Rita, you call the children? How them pickney? Them all right? How is school?" Because he was very—and always—concerned about his children. This was something I had doubted from time to time, when he'd gone into one of his disappearing acts. But he never failed to provide for them, and I learned that Bob was one father that you could close your eyes and know that Daddy's going to make it work. He always looked out for them, and not any special one but all of them.

Phone calls sort of took care of the children, but I missed my garden, too, and my akee and salt fish, and my porridge in the mornings. To offset these cravings on that first tour, we had Gilly—a juice man and a good cook, who would fry fish, or make us some bammies, just to keep our taste buds going. And we learned to travel with our Jamaican seasonings like scallions and peppers.

We worked in Europe mainly, for about three months, and when we came back, oh, I was so happy to be home! Though missing your kids may not be fun, at the end of the tour it's great when you're able to bring a suitcase full of presents for them! And when you reach home, the first thing— "Mommy, what did you bring for me?" Because I always enjoyed looking for presents, pretty things for them, for the house, for myself, for my friends and my workers.

By then we had started making *good* money. After the first tour in Europe, when we realized that we had dollars, I said to Bob, "Why don't you send your mother some money?"

He looked confused and said, "For what?"

I said, "For no reason, just for a surprise." Because Aunty had brought us up like that, when you make money, you share. Buy a bread or something. And that first tour brought us more money than we'd ever seen. So Bob did send his mother some, and she was so happy—she called to say, "I knew you did that, Rita." I also made sure that his other children got their support, that their mothers didn't have to come and hang around and ask. None of them can say they were ever deprived of child support. Eventually, though, it was easier to take some of those children into our household. The way I thought of it was, if you have to check for their dentist, and their school, and their this and their that, you might as well just give Bob and me a cool head, give us less stress. It could be confusing, it could be just too much for us to deal with every weekend. When we decided to keep them, their mothers came to visit at Hope Road, and they would sit there and play with the children, and say, "Oh, they grow big," and "Hi, Miz Marley," or "Hi, Sister Rita" when they saw me. In our relationships I was always seen as the mother figure, the caretaker, even though some rumored, "Oh she wears the ring, but I have the man," and those kinds of stories. But after a certain point there were so many I couldn't have cared less, and I'd think, that's my husband, whatever . . .

I never questioned what I was doing in this respect. I guess I carried my cross, but it seemed more about true love. About what Bob was doing, I didn't approve, but I had no control over it. I know I tried to be a good mother and provide for my children. Most of the baby mothers were local girls, neighbor girls, maybe a one-night stand here or there, as far as I knew it wasn't anything said to be a relationship. Sometimes Bob said he didn't know how it had happened—crazy! But he always respected them and saw them as women, "and man mus have nuff women," he'd say. Again Aunty was a great support, and helped to bring up the kids, though she thought it strange and couldn't understand why I was doing it.

Then, between tours, Bob began seeing Cindy Breakspeare regularly. Cindy had been one of Chris Blackwell's kittens, already living at Hope Road, with her brother, when Bob got the place. Chris had these little pussycats as his conveniences and she fell right into Bob's hand as his tenant; she was actually paying him rent for a while. As much as I knew about her then, she came from one of those families in Jamaica who would rear their daughters for men who had money. They took trips, were available for weekends, they had their lifestyle. So Bob really came in to save Cindy, because he liked her, noticed that she was a *nice* girl, and helped to turn her life around. She was really going to be Miss . . . Whatever. Bob gave her ambition. He was like that—this was another good thing about Bob—he was always real to women, always one to say, "I see more in you than you are showing." He said that to me, too.

Cindy was one of the women in his life that I couldn't, and still can't, understand. First of all, I didn't like that name: Cin-dy. I'm very funny with names. When I heard about Cindy I said, "Bob, why you and this girl, Sindy?" I was speaking to him as my buds now, because we had reached the stage where we were real friends and could speak like this, because the wife and husband thing could have gone into a divorce long before. So we had overcome that, although we still maintained our relationship as the primary one. And so I said to my friend, my buds, "What the hell is this Sindy? That's strange. Maybe she should change her name."

And Bob said, "What you talkin' about? You always carry things way out!"

I said, "Because I don't think I like that name 'Sin-dy.' And if you're going to be going with Sin-dy with an 'S' or a 'C,' stay away from me." That's how I felt at the time. I was very straightforward with him. And he knew that, which is why sometimes he'd say, "Hey gal, you feisty." I do tend to be feisty sometimes, I guess. It's my only way of showing my hurt. Back then, as today, I knew I was black and beautiful—and I was proud. Like the slogan: "Say it loud, I'm black and I'm proud!" What else could I be but black and proud around all the light-skinned "book pretty" girls?

I remember being at Hope Road one day, when Cindy lived there as Bob's tenant, and he was there, and they were carrying on their relationship. I saw her but felt calm about it, knowing that I wasn't going to make any strife. If Bob wants that, fine; if Bob likes her—that's his heart, he's having a good time, fine. But I was hurt, I guess that's normal. I remember her looking at me, and she knew I knew what was going on. But she also knew that he comes home to eat, and see his wife and children, and he stays by her sometimes. And she knows how he relies on me to keep his family together, and makes excuses about late rehearsals.

On tours sometimes we'd go shopping, and he would say to me, "Rita, Cindy asked me to bring some things for her, for the shop." And I'd say, "That's nice." But sometimes—for whatever reason, being angry at him for one thing or another, or just to test his feeling for me—I'd say, "Let me have some," just to see how he'd react. And he'd say, "Of course, have some, or all of it if you want!" For peace . . . all for peace!

Women like Cindy could be a threat to your relationship, they could really take your man, and of course that is their intention. They were the ones who said, of me, "But she's so *ordinary*. Why she doesn't do this? Why she doesn't do that? She's so *ordinary*." I was quick to realize those women were different; it wasn't like they just "had eyes for him." They were not about to be in a situation where a woman can be, as we now say in Jamaica, "your matey"—where you and another woman are dating the same man and you can maybe be "friends." But after that one scene with Esther Anderson, I never again got myself into a position of arguing with a woman over him, never. I'm a fighter, but certain things I don't fight about (though I may get sarcastic). I even began to like Cindy eventually. She would turn up at concerts in different parts of the world, and when she became pregnant, I was happy because Bob was happy.

But another thing I'll say for Bob is that he never allowed any of these women to act disrespectfully to me. Maybe that scene with Esther Anderson taught him something too—that Rita could go crazy if she wanted to. And sometimes he used me as an example of his kind of woman. Once he told one of them that she should see my *legs*—how fit I am, because I train. And she told me! He'd said to her, "You look at Rita's legs because her legs is strong like a lion!"

So when I looked at all these others, I was aware that the respect was always still there for me. He himself still gave me the manners and the respect to a certain level. I didn't think I should disrupt his relationships, though sometimes the situation was painful and I couldn't understand what was going on. But I got tired of standing in the way, and as long as I was respected, given whatever I needed financially, and whatever the kids needed was there, I let him be. If it was just about who he had sex with, he could have sex with the whole world if that was what he wanted!

I was always that type with him. I loved him as much as any of them, or more, and he knew he could count on me and depended on that loyalty, on my being his sister. But he also knew I wasn't there for the glamour, the fantasy, or the fame. That I would bring him up to reality, because I was there from the beginning, from one underpants, and those were my hands, every night, washing them out.

S OME FOOTAGE OF me appears in one of the documentaries about Bob that have come out in recent years. You see it right after a shot of him in the back of the bus, surrounded by a group of people laughing and talking. Then there's this cut to me—the sun shining on a small, black woman with a scarf around her hair, alone and leaning against a window. I think I look "cool," in terms of my mood in an environment. Something must have been going on that I was thinking about, or more likely I was in a meditative, way-out state. I can be very quiet at times, and when you're on the road—Babylon by Bus (that's the name of one album)—sometimes you really need to just hold a meditation for positive guidance and protection, because the work that we had been doing with Bob, I know the Devil didn't like it! It was like musical warfare—good against evil!

For seven years we traveled like that. I sang backup for him because I loved him, and believed in his work and felt that what he was doing was—there's no other word for it but *great*. It must be true, this greatness, that's how I've analyzed it, it was more than the flesh, it was something more like fate. Still, like Marcia and Judy, I was, in a way, invisible. Typically of that time, background vocalists weren't put on the billing, not mentioned in any promotions or publicity anywhere. The billing remained "Bob Marley and the Wailers," and we were just *there,* although sometimes the publicists might say, "Oh, the voices of the I-Three are so good," or something equally inconsequential. Though we always performed with Bob and the band, and even were featured later on as an opening act, our group never became "Bob Marley and the I-Three."

Still, if we didn't go on, Bob wouldn't go on, because we were part of the light for his stage, the icing on the cake for each night's performance. And that had to happen, even though he and I might have quarreled beforehand. (As the song says, "One good thing about music, when it hits you you feel no pain.") The I-Three were very important where Bob and his music were concerned, because his position was "This is the picture as is, this is what makes it sound this way, this is how we create character." We were also dancing and creating inspiration for *him,* and he depended on that energy to boost his individuality just as it happened. Whatever we did, we did it naturally and often spontaneously. We didn't rehearse steps, deciding, "We're all gonna do this," and so on. We might work on something, for example "turn left or right . . . you in the middle, you can do something there." But our emphasis was not on dance moves, we focused on singing and making sure the harmonies worked or else we were in big trouble. I was the one in charge of that, always seen as the leader of the group, and if anything went wrong I was expected to know why or who was at fault. When it came to the I-Three it was showtime, and since Bob relied on me to make sure that aspect was taken care of, I was always there for it. Rita the responsible.

So of course he would get on *me* at times when things went wrong. I would always get the blame. He'd say, "You didn't hear? The harmony wasn't right tonight. What happened?"

"I don't know, I sang right; you didn't hear me?"

"You, Rita . . . You should come to my room for rehearsal after the show, okay?"

And that would start an argument, with the pressure on me. So we always tried to give him our best and work out the problem, and then he'd be satisfied. "Oh, it's right," or "That's how it mus sound, that's it, now it's happening," or "Oh you girls is nice . . ." But he was very keen on his stage work with sound. As I've said, everyone was led by his musical instincts. We all gave him that respect.

Offstage, as time went on, I sometimes felt that Bob had begun to resent me, as if I might be telling him something he didn't want to hear, or acting a certain way, out of revenge. He didn't say things directly, but I could feel what was happening, because these other women came around and they'd stay up to talk or whatever. For a time he had Pascalene, a princess from Gabon, traveling with us. She followed the bus in her limousine, and sometimes he rode with her. And there I'd be in the bus. The things he did in private did less harm, but when everything was out in the open, that was really hurtful. Sometimes Pascalene and her entourage would arrive in Jamaica on her private jet and spend days. And I'd wonder, what is Bob doing with his life? What should I do? What *can* I do? I did what I could.

As for Marcia and Judy, we were sisters, oh yes. Always ready with girlfriend talk, and not always about me, because we all had our problems as young women. As far as my situation went, they were always in sympathy. They were so sweet, they'd say, "Oh no, you don't deserve some of this shit." And "How you really stand this?" But then I was made for the job, I think.

At the same time, my kids were home trying to understand why Mommy and Daddy had to go to work and leave them with Aunty, who was getting old. We had switched them to Vaz Prep, where Mrs. Ulet, the headmistress, was very helpful; unlike at other schools, it made no difference to her that Bob and the family were Rastas. Still, I'd get letters: "Oh

Aunty's getting miserable, Mommy, I can't even watch the TV. Past eight o'clock she shuts it off!"

The I-Three were seen as positive role models, with me always in the middle. Sometimes I stayed singing with tears in my eyes from certain situations I was faced with. I'd think, why keep it up? I'm gonna get off this road and go home and stay with my children. But then I'd think that if I did that, I'd be breaking up such a *good* thing that was positive to so many others all over the world. Take your troubles to the Lord and not to the people, I'd tell myself. So I did just that—I prayed. And I gave my part, I gave it honestly. I gave my part, from the heart, and I was paid for it. Paid every week, just like everybody else. So I could maintain myself, not just physically, but with a lot of spirit. And on good days, even though I wasn't altogether happy, I felt *so* independent, thinking, well, now I can do whatever I want, now I can buy clothes and shoes that I like, I can be—*whew*—just what I wanna be!

It was on one of our tours that I first met my sisters Diana and Jeanette, who were born in Stockholm. They had been news to me years before when we couldn't find Papa for a while, and the next thing we saw was a letter coming from Sweden. I remember asking Aunty, "Now where's Sweden?" And her reply: "Oh it's way *way* past Germany." By the time he and Bob met, Papa had these two beautiful daughters, and I imagine they followed Bob's career closely after that. Their mother, even though she could barely speak English, would call me to ask when we were coming to Stockholm for a concert, because we usually performed there. So we developed a relationship, and whenever we were coming Diana and Jeanette were the excitement of Stockholm, because everybody knew they were going to the concert and were going to meet me at my hotel. They'd come with their friends, and it was fun to look at them, just saying wow, look at that! Sisters! You could see they had some Jamaican in them, you could see the mixture. They're singers also, these days they're one of the top pop groups in Stockholm, and we still communicate and see each other. They go by their mother's name, Soderholm, and they sing facing each other, like twins.

Those seven years spent touring Europe, Africa, and America alternated with studio work for albums and some peaceful times in Bull Bay and other times that no one could ever have anticipated. Though Bob and I had agreed to be friends, and I dealt well enough with his womanizing, I still had to deal with his possessive attitude toward me, which he never gave up no matter what I said or did. This put more pressure on me than I wanted. Even though he was carrying on right under my nose (mostly one-night stands), he remained very suspicious of my having an affair: "You can't tell me you're not doing this, you're not doing that!"

When we argued, my line was always, "Who cares? I'm your wife but I'm not your slave, you know? I'm not gonna be your call girl, when you want to have sex you call me to your room? Or we have a relationship *when you feel like?* No no no! And I'm not having a relationship with you going around with all these women—every city you have to hit on somebody? Miss Brussels? Miss Miami Beach? No no no!!"

When we started touring, Tacky was still helping Aunty take care of the kids. Sometimes he'd call me to say everything's fine and let me know what's happening, or I'd call him and ask him to look in on everyone and call me afterward. As I've said, he was my very good friend. But then Bob would look at my phone bill when we were checking out of the hotels; he would always tell the promoter, "Get me Rita's bill." Yes, he was like that— you wouldn't imagine that he could be so jealous of me, he was *so* jealous of me, even the guys in the band couldn't believe it. To this day, Minnie shakes her head over how irrational this was.

I remember a scene with Neville Garrick, Tuff Gong's (the name of Bob's recording company) lighting designer, that happened one evening during a U.S. tour. Bob had brought Yvette Anderson along on the tour.

Earlier, when we had checked into the hotel, she had smiled at me and I'd smiled back, and then we all went to our rooms. Later on I'd wanted a smoke, so I called Neville and asked him to bring me some. When Bob came in, as he usually did, Neville was there, and when Bob saw him he had a fit, shouting, "What you doin' in here?"

Neville said, "Rita just asked me for a little spliff . . ."

Without another word Bob just lifted me up out of the bed, yelling—"*Raahh!*"—and held me up in the air, and then dropped me down! And Neville was so frightened! After Bob left the room he said, "Oh, now he's going to send me home!"

I said, "Oh no, he wouldn't . . ." But poor Neville! He was so humble, just bringing a little smoke to cool me—only for sympathy, knowing that Yvette was with Bob, and right in front of my eyes. But Bob had to go and create that big excitement, even though Neville, like all the band members, had always offered only love and respect for me. But Bob was nevertheless always very jealous and very watchful, very *sneaky*. I never understood how somebody could be like that.

At home, though, he was busy with his business at Hope Road. And I had a chance to rest and get back into my family. Touring and performing can exhaust the strongest person, even if you're young and enthusiastic about what you're doing, even though you love it and know that it's what you're cut out to do. But there was much at home that interested me too. The farm in Clarendon was still in operation, and Minnie was around to help with that. Bob remained very supportive of it, and there were days when he'd drive us to the farm just to get the produce. Sometimes we'd go there and stay overnight with him. Bob loved farming and taught me a lot about planting food. It was so peaceful to be away from everyone and we had a building there to relax in, a three-bedroom house that had come with the farm. We also had a big outdoor kitchen, where he would do the cooking. Those times, when I'd get his undivided attention, were always special to me.

I couldn't have done any of this without Aunty there running the show with Miss Collins. Without Aunty, I could never have moved that well, if at all. Every way she was strict with the children I approved of, because she wasn't going to see certain things happen. I could see her work in me, and wanted as much for them. And in Jamaica times were changing—slowly—for women. Despite their complaints when I was away, the children liked to see me work when I was home. My work enhanced their lives, I think: "This is what Mommy says, these are things that Mommy does." They were growing big now; except for Stephanie, who was still a baby, they were all in school. I thought it was very important that they knew what Mommy did, and that they supported her. Sometimes they'd remind me, "Mommy, it's Friday, aren't you going to your farm today? Is Daddy going? Can we go with you?" We did things like that, so that we would have time together. Bob loved those weekends, as he loved his children. They were his true friends, he always said.

When I wasn't around, there were people who took care of the Queen of Sheba Restaurant for me. Minnie especially. When we were at home in Jamaica and working at the studio there, she'd come to rehearsals to keep us company and bring us juice or food, always offering opinions about the music: "This one is not going to be Number One, but that one is." Because she and I were so close, and so militant, many rumors were spread about us. We're both early morning persons, and back then we liked to go for a morning run together, so even if we woke up at four o'clock in the morning, we'd call each other. Our children used to get so angry at us because they knew why the phone was ringing—it was me calling Minnie or her calling me. Bob knew better than to believe the rumors (which mostly concerned our sexuality); still, he refused to believe that I actually *did* go running with Minnie at 5 A.M. around the local reservoir (which is about four miles in circumference, and we sometimes did two or three laps). One morning Bob paid a surprise visit and of course found us there. But at least he demonstrated his goodwill and fitness by running along with us—though he only made one lap and couldn't believe we were able to do three easily!

People often took Minnie for Bob's sister, because they had similar complexions, and he always said they had the same foreheads and cheekbones. Anywhere we went together they would just pick her out and ask, is that his sister, and he'd say, "Yeah, mon." He admitted to me that "some brethren come tell me a lot of things about you and Minnie," but to her he said, "I know you more than that, I know you're my sister, and you a Rasta."

Most people were scared of Bob when he got mad, because, as Minnie says, he could get very rough, very tough. I remember someone asking Minnie, "Is that your brother?" She just didn't want to say right out, "Yes, he's my brother," because she felt that he was a big star and she was just there in the supportive group. So she said, instead, "He's my brother in Rastafari." And he looked around and said to her, good and loud, "What the bloodclaat is this 'brother in Rastafari'! The man ask if you's my sister, say yes or no!"

Minnie defended and comforted me, was always the friend I could tell certain things to, one of those who would say to me, "Oh don't worry . . ." Through her I met Angela Melhado, another runner. The three of us have been running around Jamaica for almost thirty years now. Angie and Minnie grew up on opposite sides of the same uptown road in Kingston—Minnie says Angie's wealthy parents were like her Santa Claus. Years later they remet on the track at the reservoir, and then the three of us began running together. We swim, too. To this day, we love the river; anywhere there's water on the island of Jamaica—in the bush, in the mountains—we three find it and go swimming. We go all about in this country, because we know it's beautiful and special. And we love the same things—we love to pray, we love helping people out. Angie and Minnie paint drug rehab centers and things like that.

Back then, Angie was living outside the city on her property in the mountains. Like me, she loved to grow things. The day Minnie brought her to Hope Road to meet Bob, she came with a beautiful straw hamper packed with every little thing from her garden. She had put the basket on the ground when Bob came out of the house, and in the course of the introductions she said, "Well, I brought this basket." He looked down at it and said, "What's in it?" And Angie said, "Well, I've been growing these vegetables and I wanted you to have them." Bob just kind of looked off at her, with his head cocked to one side. He appreciated that so much, because he was always giving to people, and people hardly ever gave *him* things. So he was a little taken aback, I think, and just stood there, with his head to the side, eyeing her, and saying, "Nice, nice. Give thanks, man."

Whenever Minnie came on tour with us, she'd help with my clothes and stuff, but more often she helped with the food, and from that experience, in the mid-seventies she opened Minnie's Health Food Restaurant, also on Hope Road, with cuisine derived from the ideas we'd been trying to present at the Queen of Sheba. Everyone would find themselves there at lunchtime, gossiping over some of the most wonderful dishes, from food in coconut milk to rundown (coconut milk boiled down to gravy), made with all the best fresh things you can think of, because as always Minnie got up early and was first at the market. Neither of us was in this food business just for the money; we were trying to make poor people see a lifestyle, a way of living that was simple but healthy. It didn't take much, but it took the best. And that's what we did. In Jamaica we have a saying, that a person should take the sour and turn it into sweet. We took the sour and we made lemonade!

In 1975, Minnie helped me make Bob's first-ever birthday party. We put together a big spread at the Queen of Sheba. In all his life—all his thirty years!—he had never before had a birthday party. He cried a little at that party—even though there were plenty of babies to do the crying, Minnie's kids and mine, all his other children. Judy Mowatt came with her kids, some band members were there too. Bob told everyone that this was his first birthday ever. We had a great time, and in Jamaica since 1981 we continue to celebrate February 6 as Bob Marley Day.

So many of Bob's lyrics reflect our personal life, from "Nice Time" to "Chances Are" to "Stir It Up," which he wrote when I came back from Delaware. And, of course, "No Woman No Cry." Sometimes, on tour, if we'd had an argument before the show and he wanted to apologize, while we were performing that song he'd use the opportunity to come over to me onstage and put his arm around my shoulder, with sometimes a kiss or a whisper "I love you" in my ear.

I could go on and on about what song meant what, because basically when Bob wrote he didn't always write alone, but sometimes with Bunny or Peter or Vision or his other friends feeling a drum sound, or humming a piece. He relied on me for different kinds of advice at the end of the day. He might call to say, "Did you read what I did last night; it's on the table." Or "How does this sound?" Or "Did I spell this right?" Or "Was that the right way to say it?" So that most of the lyrics you come across, especially in the early times, pertained to the life we shared. I don't want to make it seem as if I'm claiming them, but we did a lot of writing together. Sometimes we'd go into the Bible for verses or psalms. In the little cellar studio at Bull Bay—those were some of the times when he would really go into his soul. Bob always wanted his lyrics to give a positive message of love, peace, and unity. And he would come out the next day with "Wow, we could do this one." And he would take it from there to the next step.

At some point during the touring years, although the fight was in there and the trouble war existed, we were getting along and had begun living as man and wife again. This was about the time we took in Karen, who was born in London and whose mother had taken her to Jamaica to live with her grandmother (the baby's great-grandmother). The mother had left and then told Bob "the baby's in Jamaica"; I guess she was trying to get Karen as close as possible, to make sure Bob provided for her. Typical Jamaican girl (and I can't exclude myself—to some extent). Mother always ends up with the baby!

When Bob said to me, "I have a daughter in Harbour View," I was a bit surprised, at the location more than the fact. He said, "You need to go look at her," and I could tell he might be worried, so I agreed. When I got there, the great-grandmother said to the child, "Here's your mother." The little girl, who was about four or five, very shy and obviously not happy, said, "Mommy," and when I was leaving, after having spoken with the great-grandmother for a while, she started to cry. When I got home I told Bob that I thought we should take her because it didn't seem to me that the great-grandmother could manage her. "And let her and Stephanie grow up together," I said, "because Karen is one year older, and Stephanie is the smallest among the big ones, so she and Karen would be company for each other."

By now he was used to my thinking like this. Still, he said, "Do you really mean that?" I said, "Of course." So we took Karen to live with us, and she and Stephanie, and Stephen because he was also close in age, grew up like triplets. They became quite a team. Karen was the leader and Stephanie always followed her. Sometimes, if I had three or four days off while on tour, I'd fly home to see everyone. One night at 9 P.M. I arrived unexpectedly to find that Karen and Stephanie weren't there. I called the police, everyone I knew, all their friends, we even went on a search. We were all so worried—I almost lost my mind! We found them with friends early the next afternoon, too scared to come home because it had been so late, and no one had expected that I'd be home to make such a fuss!

In many ways, during most of those touring years, though I traveled all over the world, I remained at the same place mentally that I'd been the day Bob's driver arrived talking about "an emergency." Every once in a while, when I was home, I'd say to Marcia and Judy, "Sorry, you girls can continue, but I'm thinking very much of getting out of this and leaving him alone." Because between tours Marcia had her career and Judy had hers, but my life was still tied up in Bob's and I felt unfulfilled and sometimes used. When I told him that I needed to really do something for myself, he was very supportive; I knew he felt sorry for me and knew what I was feeling and how I must be thinking—Bob was very honest with me. He even wrote a song for me to sing: "Play Play Play" ("All you do is just play play play"). Oh he understood (somewhat), because he had a lot of dreams for me in terms of what he wanted me to be. If I complained sometimes about the other baby mothers, he'd say, "Baby, you couldn't have all the babies that I feel I should have. I don't want to get you pregnant every year. So some of that is really just taking the burden off you and your body." That was one of his lines, "taking the burden off you." "Because I know you have to work," he'd say, "I know you *want* to work. I know you have to sing."

But then, when the possibility of my working solo did arise, he was less understanding than controlling. That opportunity wasn't presented until the very late seventies, when an offer came from Hansa Music, a French company. When the I-Three worked as an opening act for the group, each one of us got to solo. Bob was making statements and attracting attention in the overseas media, so the Hansa people came to see our show one night in France and said, "Oh Rita, you could do the same, your voice is so good and your albums will be great, let's do promotions on it." They thought that in me they saw something *big*. Frank Lipsik, the head of the company, and Catherine Petrowsky, their public relations person, came down to Jamaica and we met. Frank Lipsik was really excited—he began calling me every day to say, "We're coming for you, we want to bring you to Paris!" Oh, they were going to do great big things. So of course I was very interested. I knew, also, that it was important for me to try *by myself*.

But Bob said, "Oh no, that's not what should be happening."

"But this is my thing!" I said.

"If you're gonna do something, let it stay in the family," he insisted. "You don't want no white man to come steal your business. This is family! Why are you doing this? Why don't you continue to give me a hand while we're trying to form our own thing? Why don't you wait? Let me get a break; then after my break I'll give you a break."

But I said, "Your break is your break, and I feel I'm being stifled, because I know I have the ability." And in spite of his disapproval, I agreed to do an album for this company and began sending them cassettes as we went along with the album production. As for Bob, I thought, he'll be mad, but at the same time, hey hey hey—I can sing!

When he found out, he was happy for me but still not in favor of it and said, "I don't like this."

And I'm saying, *Uh-oh* . . . Because they had given me a five-thousand-dollar advance, which in those days was big money. I said to him, "Look, this is my check! And it's for the album! So I have a commitment." I went ahead with it and went to Paris for interviews; Hansa sent photographers to Clarendon for photo sessions. They were all over me; they were very good. At one point they sent me to Sweden for radio and TV promotions, because the record was soon going to be released in that country. And there, waiting at the airport, was my father! Papa had got word that I was coming and had been looking out for me. It had been so many years, but there he was—I couldn't believe it! And we hugged, and oh, he took me here and there, we took pictures, and the next day our story was all over the newspaper: "Lost Father Found in Sweden." That was the first time I'd seen him since I had gone running from Delaware to Brooklyn to him and Miss Alma. I spent about four or five days with him, and we were so happy to see each other. I loved Papa. It was hard, after missing him and seeing him again, to leave him. I wasn't to see him again until Bob's funeral.

The album I was making for Hansa was to be called *Who Feels It Knows It*, and some of their people came down for the last sessions. We did one photo shoot and the next day were supposed to be going out to the country to do another when Bob chased the publicist away! I think he was a little bit crazy with jealousy at that point. He started shouting at her, "Get out of here and leave her alone! *I* will sign her! *I* will promote her! You're *using* her, you want to take her away . . ."

Catherine Petrowsky, who was a lovely young woman, cried like a baby. She said, "No, Bob, that's not the point. Rita is her own individual self and she can *be*. She has the talent, she can be what she wants to be."

I felt *so* sorry for that white girl. But he walked her out, telling her, "Leave my wife alone. Leave my wife alone!" It was a devastating experience and I was furious and ashamed. But we were about to leave on tour, and I couldn't do anything about it then.

Bob must have known, though, that I wouldn't let the matter rest. And, fortunately, neither did Catherine Petrowsky. In Europe she turned up at every concert, polite but determined just to see me and let me do interviews for my album. Without fighting with Bob, the two of us worked on him. We met with him, explained that I was doing great and the deal was on. Finally, one night in Brussels, we wore him down. He looked at Catherine, eye to eye, and said, "Hansa . . . is the answer . . . for Rita!" So eventually I did go into a deal with them. And, sadly, during Bob's illness I was on promotions for this album when I had to leave to go to him. I went from the promotions to the hospital. And his mother said, "Why your career now, all of a sudden your career, just when he don't want that around him?"

I tried to explain that this was something I couldn't help, that it was something that had been set in motion a good while before he got sick. But in the end, although I didn't want to drop it, I felt I had to anyway. Bob's health was my priority. I suppose I should see it as ironic, but to me it's just sad that these moments coincided, that Bob would be leaving me just about the time that I was about to make my way as an individual performer, into a career as more than just a background singer. There was more to our lives, though, before all of that happened.

chapter eleven
WAR

I N T H E F A L L of 1976, with an election scheduled, the crime rate in
Jamaica was high, tensions were running high, and the government had
been unable to bring any stability to certain areas of Kingston. We had
been independent since 1962, and black people finally had the right to
vote, but many of Jamaica's poor were still suffering, not only in city ghettos like Trench Town but in rural areas like St. Ann. Both major political
parties, the Jamaica Labour Party (JLP) and the People's National Party
(PNP), continued to make promises they couldn't keep and continued to
use the rude boys for their own purposes. When it was time for politics,
the party bosses would hand out guns and say, "Go kill the opposition."
After elections, they'd be unable to take these guns back, because the boys
were now gun crazy, possessed. So you'd find these street toughs, or whatever name you want to call them, with guns in their hands. And the war
continued.

By this time we had been touring long enough to be known all over the
world, which only added to Bob's already existing reputation in Jamaica. At

home he was seen as "the voice of the people," and the ghetto youth were very aware of this. Despite his move uptown, they still regarded him very highly. The biggest murderers, the biggest gunmen, would come to him for help. Hope Road became a welfare center—there was no night there, twenty-four hours a day they'd arrive demanding to see him. He'd become more important than the prime minister. It began to seem as if he had to live *for* them. Added to this, he was subjected to certain pressures from one party or the other, and it was risky to be in the middle. He was living a very dangerous life, simply because he had brought all this attention to the island of Jamaica through his music. It can be nice to be on top, but not when some heavy burdens settle on your shoulders. You may be up there, but you're also out there. Bob had no time for himself, and no privacy.

It reached the point where people preyed on him, people who felt that he had to have them around, for "protection," for one thing, because "somebody might try to kill you." And for another thing, you might be able to help them financially, which he always did. So they had reasons to be hanging around, to have their prey in view. In one of Bob's songs, he sings, "Too much mixup, gotta clear my wheels, once and for all, I gotta clear my wheels, I don't care who falls, because it's too much mixup." He became paranoid and found himself waking up every morning just waiting for these people to come and get him. And faced with that sort of thing, I'm saying, "Keep it out of the family house, away from the children . . ." There were times when we slept on the floor because we had to give up our beds to people who needed to hide out from other gangs.

Eventually—inevitably—he was targeted to help bring stabilization to the country, to appease the ghetto youth. The government said, "Bob, it's only you who can say it through your music. Let us have a concert." It was a peace concert they wanted, to be called "Smile Jamaica," in order to calm everyone down before the elections that were to be held in December. Bob invited Peter and Bunny as the original Wailers to perform, but they refused. Peter said he wanted no peace, he wanted equal rights and justice. Bunny said no because the event was political and he wouldn't participate. The concert, sponsored by the Jamaica Ministry of Culture, would be free. At first it had been planned for Jamaica House, but I had a dream that we should change the venue; I told Bob, and he arranged for it to be held at the National Heroes Circle in Kingston.

We were still so young—Bob was thirty-one and I was thirty. At that age, in such a high-profile position, in a business full of producers and managers and handlers and what have you, you were not always able to say "Well, no, no thank you" on your own. You were always being advised, and other people's decisions were so often considered to be "what is right for you." And even *with* a roomful of advisers, Bob was still caught up in certain situations that had less to do with his career than with his social and political position.

And so he decided to do the concert, even though we realized how dangerous it had become. It was scheduled for Sunday, December 5, 1976, but instead of something for the people, it became something for the politicians. And Bob was being used. Rumor had it that he was doing this for the party in power, the PNP, when that was not so. Then this drew some action from the opposition, and he was warned not to do the concert because they were going to kill him. The whole week before, regulars at Hope Road noticed strangers on the premises from time to time. Bob got caught up in this and it was terrible, the divisions and the contradictions. But he was determined to do the show for the people who suffered the most.

The Friday afternoon before the concert, while we were rehearsing, we heard what sounded like firecrackers, and I said to myself why firecrackers, it's not Christmas—though sometimes we do have Chinese New Year, so it might be . . . Later, toward evening, I had just said good-bye to Bob because I had to go to another rehearsal that night with the drama group I was in, which I kept up with when we weren't touring and was scheduled to present a musical called *Brashana "O."* I'd said to him, "See you later," and he'd said, "Okay, take care . . ."

Shanty and Senior, two young men from the neighborhood, had come to town with me from Bull Bay, and they were waiting in my car to go home. As I got into the front seat and turned around to greet them, I saw some guys I didn't recognize on the stairs to the second floor I'd just left. They had guns in their hands. I thought, oh no, and quickly started the car, a nice, loud Volkswagen—*bwap bwap bwap bwap*—just as they began firing wildly. The sound of the motor distracted one guy, who half turned around as he got off a shot toward where I knew Bob was speaking with Don Taylor, his manager. Then the gunman turned back toward me. I stepped hard on the gas pedal, *vroooom*, but he and some others came after the car as it began moving—I guess they couldn't tell who was driving out. I put that pedal to the floor, trying to get away, but then bullets started flying through the car, from the rear, like crazy . . .

The youths in back fell to the floor yelling, "Duck, Mommy, duck duck!" I bent as low as I dared over the steering wheel and kept driving until I felt a warm thing coming down my neck and I thought, shit, I'm dead! I'm dead, because a bullet hit my head.

So I stopped a little way from the gate, and pulled up the emergency, and rested my head on the steering wheel, and said to myself, yes I'm dead, this is how dead feels. And I thought of Aunty and the children and wondered if they'd really killed Bob. One of the gunmen came to the car window and looked in and put his gun to my head, but then he said "Everybody dead, everybody dead" and didn't fire again.

Then the people next door started to turn on their lights, and I heard windows opening. The guy stood there a little longer. I guess he was going to make sure I was dead, but someone must have called the police, because I heard a siren. Then, with all the noise, he—and the other six I later learned about—obviously realized they had to get out of there. I kept pretending to be dead, trying not to breathe, until I heard running footsteps, and then I lifted my head a little to see men with guns running past the open gate to their car, which was parked across the entrance, blocking the gate, so I wouldn't have been able to drive out in any case.

The blood was coming through my locks and running down my face, and in the middle of telling myself I was dead all of a sudden I realized I was really still alive, and I thought, oh my God, where is Bob. I got out of the car and looked in the back for my two passengers. They were well under the seat, and I said, "They're gone, come, you can get up." But the poor guys were frozen. The whole back window of the car was shattered, nobody sitting upright could have come out of there alive. That those young men had survived was a miracle.

Bob could easily have been killed that night. Too easily. He had gone to the kitchen after I left him and had been standing there, peeling a grapefruit. The gunman who got him was aiming for the heart, but the bullet just creased his chest and hit his elbow (and stayed there for the rest of his life; he went to his resting place with it still there).

Aunty was at the house in Bull Bay with the kids, and when they heard on the radio "Bob Marley and Rita Marley have both been shot," you know they went crazy. Oh poor Aunty, just her out there with the kids . . . The police went there immediately to get them, as we didn't know what to expect next.

That was close, a close call, and Jah was so good that nobody died that night, though Don Taylor was struck by five bullets and eventually airlifted to Miami with one lodged near his spine. Everyone thought he was dead and wouldn't touch him, but Bob lifted him up and put him in a car along with me, and Diane Jobson drove us quickly to the hospital. When we got there, the doctors didn't operate on me right away because they said they couldn't touch the bullet immediately, that it was too near the brain. So they had to allow it to settle and wait for the swelling to go down, and since this would take a few days, I was admitted to the hospital under police guard. When Aunty and the kids came to see me, everyone was crying.

On Sunday, though, I was onstage, singing, because Bob decided to go ahead and do the concert. Come what may, he said, they could kill him now, but he was going to do it for the people. Some members of the band refused to play, so other musicians came together. Judy was also there with me to do background, though Marcia had gone to New York; she had been warned not to perform from early on, she said, so she had flown out. Bob stood there, out in the open, exposed to whatever might happen, his arm in a sling, unable to play guitar. I was still in my hospital jacket, my head all bandaged up and everything. And we sang.

I know those shots changed me, and they changed Bob too. After that he was frightened, though at the concert he bravely rolled up his sleeve to show his wounds to the crowd and reenacted the shooting in a dance. But now he was frightened in a way he hadn't been, because even though he'd been warned by these gunmen that they were out to get him, he never thought they would try. And all of us now knew that with no trouble at all they could succeed, and how little it would take for them to try again.

Everything went down the drain then, everything, because nobody could have anticipated the situation we were now in. I went back to Bull Bay after that just to pack some things and get us out of Jamaica; this was so unreal. When you discover that somebody will try to kill you, you have to start thinking differently. So plans had to change. Bob and the kids and I, along with Neville Garrick, went to Nassau to live for a while, in one of Chris Blackwell's homes there. I called Bob's mother and she came down from Delaware to help out and stayed a few days.

At the time of the shooting, Cindy Breakspeare had just won the 1976 Miss World title. I hadn't even known that Chris Blackwell had sponsored her to the contest, but Bob had and was a little more prepared for the eventuality of her winning. After she won they'd been planning to do a movie to be called *Beauty and the Beast*. So she soon arrived in Nassau, and

I suppose they abandoned their plans to make the movie, because I never heard of it again. She wouldn't dare stay where we were, of course, but she came in from London and stayed in a hotel, and he would visit her there. Cindy—and Cindy's mother, it was later revealed—had expectations that were never fulfilled. I guess like any young girl she wanted to get married and was acting on the premise that this would eventually happen. Her mother asked Cedella Booker, "Why doesn't Bob get his divorce? He promised Cindy that they were going to get married, and he's still living with Rita!"

But Moms just said, "Uh-uh, just stop there, don't touch that line." Because although she was interested in Bob's different relationships and the girls that he would bring to see her, she always gave me that love and respect.

Married or not, Bob then went into exile in England, where Cindy was living. And I realized that oh, this was going to happen eventually. As for me, I couldn't stay in Nassau indefinitely, and there were the children to think of, who had to go to school, so I brought them back to Jamaica, to Bull Bay. But after such violence, I didn't feel safe.

It's hard to describe how I felt during this time, knowing that I would have to leave my house and garden, and trying to recover from my injury (the doctors said my thick dreadlocks saved my life). And like another, invisible wound was my grief and confusion about what was happening, with Bob off living in England. By then he was really *living* in England as well as doing studio work; it was living in exile or whatever, but he was living there. I felt tossed and turned, as if everything had started to shuffle. I would wake in the morning thinking nothing was right, wondering how long this was going to last, and if it was going to last or would it end. I kept telling myself, get ready to stand on your own two feet, you don't want to be left out in the cold, you were trained to be independent, and now you have to be. Be strong, stand up and fight.

I told Bob we'd have to move, because if I felt this way, the children felt worse, and we had to live in a secure area where we felt protected. Bob agreed, and it was Gilly, our tour cook, who said, "Yeah, man, it's scary for you to live all the way out there in Bull Bay alone with the children," and found a house for us in Kingston on Washington Drive, a few doors away from the then prime minister, Michael Manley. I rented it at first and then Bob bought it for us.

After we moved from Bull Bay into the building on Washington Drive, which was what we call a "three-sister" and Americans call a "three-family" house, Abba Mendefro and Zacgi from Ethiopia, the former a priest of the Ethiopian Orthodox Church and the latter a teacher, became our tenants there. The church couldn't afford rent, and living conditions had been diffi-cult for Abba, so he agreed to help Aunty take care of the kids. He became like a grandfather to them, and I felt so much better then. I was sure that with Abba around, Satan wouldn't dare come in that yard! The children were safe—Ziggy even became an altar boy—and it was as if my faith were being restored. So there again I was able to hold on to whatever that power was—Jah? God? Allah? Whatever name you want to use, I was able to use that power to sustain myself.

Bob and I still spoke almost every day. He would call to ask, "What you doing? What's happening with the children?" He was in the studios up there in London, and one day he said, "You know I need the I-Three, we want you all to come up to record some background vocals, because I'm here working." So I said fine, okay, we'd do that, because now that the chil-dren were safe with Aunty and Abba, I felt I could go back to work. So I called Marcia and Judy and we flew to England. And it was when I returned home that I found another message from Frank Lipsik's French company, Hansa, about this solo album they wanted from me. It seemed like a very good time for that to happen.

When Eric Clapton recorded Bob's tune "I Shot the Sheriff" and made it a big international hit, Bob got a lot of recognition as a revolutionary.

This pleased him immensely; he was happy to be known as "the musical revolutionist," fighting his war with his music. His songs seemed to reach out beyond national borders and apply to everyone's life with their meaning intact. Most of the American singers who were prominent during that time had been listening to Bob Marley. Keenly.

Stevie Wonder, for one, loved Bob's music, and he was getting to love Bob the man as well. He always said, "Bob, I want to plan a tour with you. Be the opening act for me," and that tour had been in the planning stages when Bob got sick. Stevie wrote "Master Blaster" with Bob in mind. When he came to Jamaica and we did a concert with him it was so deep, as if these men had been seeing each other for years—and I mean seeing with eyes, because even though Stevie is blind, he sees so much because he feels so much! It was as if Stevie had been seeing Bob for what he was and what he wanted to be. Roberta Flack was another one who came to Jamaica, drawn by Bob's talents. I remember being around her for a while and being aware of what a strong woman she was. Stevie, Roberta, Barbra Streisand, a lot of those people were into Bob's music.

But the music's content didn't please everyone. In the States this was a time when anyone who preached "revolution" and "peace" in any way, even musically, was subject to intense scrutiny. Now that Bob had become so well-known outside Jamaica, his impact on other political situations besides our own was being tracked. It wasn't easy to be in that position, either. I still have a package that proves that Bob's moves were being monitored by the U.S. intelligence agencies. And because he found himself the victim of a "We are watching you" situation, he had to be very discreet; he had to start watching himself. Although at the time it was difficult to prove that any such thing was happening, in later years someone was able to secure the files through the Freedom of Information Act.

Six months after the shooting, Bob decided to come home. I think he was getting bored with London, or maybe it was getting too close to winter (he wrote "Misty Morning, No See No Sun" there). But he was influenced, also, by friends in Jamaica, because there was still unrest in the country, and gang warfare. People—in the ghettos especially—were still asking for him, saying that unless Bob Marley came back to Jamaica there would be no peace. Political heavies, too, were eager for him to return, "because if the people see you . . ." By then some of the guys who had attempted the assassination had been found. So Bob returned to a hero's welcome and a great deal of excitement.

And he came back to live with us on Washington Drive, but things had changed so radically, I'd find the most dangerous men around him sometimes (he said "for protection"). And I'd be thinking, wow, they're sleeping in *my* bed? He'd come home saying, "Rita, we have to put up this guy tonight," and we'd have to sleep in the living room. I just started making my bed up and taking it down, and making it up and taking it down. It seemed as if things were left to *their* discretion mostly, not his, as if he had given himself up to them. And then I would say, "You're just like Jesus Christ, he gave his life for the people." Sometimes I still think like that—yeah, he gave it up, he gave it to them. But you could see he was no longer comfortable in Jamaica; he couldn't take it anymore, he became very paranoid and edgy. We thought of going to Ethiopia to live, but he said the Twelve Tribes organization said it wasn't his turn yet; they usually sent members by turns. I still don't understand that.

Usually, before we traveled, each of us on the tour was allowed to get a salary advance, in case we wanted to leave money for our families or anything else. Before we left on what would turn out to be our last tour, I asked for an advance, because I too wasn't feeling good living where we were. By then it was election time again, and many of Jamaica's wealthier, upper-class people were running away from the system that remained unchanged, the gang violence that once again threatened to engulf the island. And so houses were going for what seems like a small amount now—twelve thousand to thirty thousand dollars. For me that was big money in 1980. We were still talking about security being important, and I didn't want to leave the children around the Washington Drive area because, with the election imminent and us being neighbors to one of the political leaders, it didn't feel safe any longer. I wanted to buy a house I'd seen that was up on one of the hills overlooking Kingston. It was a beautiful Spanish-style building, a house on the hilltop, like the one I'd first visited when we started to work with Johnny Nash. The kids loved it. I knew I couldn't pay cash, but that something would work out.

I told Bob I'd found a home and that I wanted to set the kids up before we left. What I didn't know was that Bob had Diane Jobson's father planning a real estate thing, to build a mansion for him in Nine Miles. When I did hear about it I realized I wasn't being mentioned, that it wasn't really for me, because then Bob began to talk about having a big underground studio; he was going to stop touring and settle down with his children.

So I said to him, "Okay, you do what you want to do." He said he wanted a bigger house. But I wasn't going to give up so easily. I said, "Okay, but the one I found has a nice acreage of land, and my lawyer said, if I'm gonna choose it I have to fill out the papers before I go, because there are other people who are interested, and I should leave an advance."

I didn't push it at first, because I thought I might be getting too . . . too demanding maybe. But then I got really determined, thinking, he's not leaving me. I asked him to come up to see the place. When he arrived, with Diane Jobson, Bob looked around, and his response was that the place was nice, but it was too small for his children. So I said, "Well, it could be bigger. This is a big property. I mean, we can develop on it if you want; make more rooms when we get back from the tour."

But he said, "No, I'm not interested."

Later, when we were alone, he explained more about what he was doing in Nine Miles, which is actually where his mausoleum is now. He was preparing that place to live, he told me, because this would be his last tour, his last deal with Island Records. The contract was up, and he was to be on his own, definitely on his own with his music. So he was making a decision for his life. Where to go from here, after his last album for Chris Blackwell. He'd be a better father, spend more time with his children, he'd be a better husband, he'd be a better friend . . . blah blah blah. We laughed and talked all night. Promises, and oh . . .

"Okay, Bob," I said. "But in the meantime, I'm going to buy this house."

Before this, I was always able to keep an eye on him. And he was happy for that. I was his eye, I was his pain; when things were not right, I would be the shoulder. I created home for him anywhere I was. And he loved that. He loved to know he could get away, especially after he became public property, and *oh* they would pick on him. And when I looked at him, I'd see him getting skinny, I'd see when he started to fret, I could tell when he wasn't happy. Even the whole woman thing was becoming a problem for him. They might enjoy sex, but he wasn't enjoying his life. Sex is one thing, but what happens afterward? What can you give? What is your contribution? And that's what was lacking in most of Bob's relationships; the one-night stands were becoming physically and spiritually boring—that took a lot out of him.

The day after I had decided to buy the house on the hill, I drove up there (in the BMW Bob had bought me—I guess as a consolation—when he became more friendly with Cindy). I looked around again and said to myself, wow, I'm taking a chance. But hey, it's a positively savvy chance, I told myself, when you consider you *have* to do it, you just *have* to do it. Buy yourself a home that you love. Girl, if you don't make it happen, nobody's gonna do it for you. Make up your mind; Bob seems to be on a different trip. Something felt strange, I could feel a different vibe. But I'd been through all that. There were enemies, and it was an easy thing to have enemies. And I had friends. Just a few. Real friends were a few.

So I took the advance money for the tour and I told the manager, "Don't pay me on the road, just send the money straight to this lawyer in Jamaica." Because, after all, that was me. I'm not gonna live in the darkness, I told myself, I have to be where the light shines. And I'm gonna live in the house on the hill.

IN SEPTEMBER 1975, during a football game, one of the players wearing spikes stepped on the big toe of Bob's right foot. The injury was somewhat severe, but he refused to give it much attention, because Bob was Bob, who never gave in to pain, and a hurt toe wasn't as serious as other things that needed looking after. So he took it very lightly and continued to play on the foot even though doctors recommended that he rest it and not run around for a while. I would be the last one who saw it most evenings, when he came home and took off his sneakers and socks. He was hurt enough to complain—ouch!—and I could see the toe was not healing. I kept saying, "Bob, it's still not looking good, you have to quit wearing these kinds of shoes and give up the football for a time." He'd say okay, and he'd stop for a day or two, and the next day he'd be out on the field again.

Eventually, after he reinjured the toe in 1977, the nail fell off, and then malignant melanoma developed, ironically, a disease that rarely occurs in people of color. But Bob felt the doctors who made this diagnosis were lying, even Dr. Bacon, a black doctor in Miami who loved Bob and who said to me, "If Bob would allow me to get rid of the toe, we could stop this thing." After the doctor spoke to me I spoke to Bob about it, but Bob thought I was crazy, because he believed that if he consented to this he wouldn't be able to stand up during performances. "How would I go onstage? They won't stay looking at a crippled man!" He spoke angrily to me, as if I were being deliberately negative. So I thought, okay, this is not a time for him to feel that way about me. I felt I had to support *his* will because I didn't want him to feel as if I were trying to weaken him when he needed strength most of all.

In any case, the decision wasn't left to me. My influence was more and more limited in that hothouse, superstar atmosphere where rumors flew about his illness and people told him this and that. Naturally, I had my opinion about some of the things that were said, but I didn't try to make a fuss, to publicize my feelings.

Bob was told that Dr. Bacon was lying, that it was only a sore toe and would get better soon, that he should come out of the hospital where this diagnosis had been made. Which he did.

So that final tour went on, and we traveled from one country to another, one city to another, doing the same thing we had done for almost seven years. Night after night, city after city, crowds of fans—thousands of people—came out to see Bob; for them he had become more than just a singer; they wanted to hear the message in his music, what he had to say. Along with this every aspect of his life was inspected—whatever he did, whatever he thought, whatever others thought of him.

This meant an openness, with many more people having access to him. When he became that accessible, because of the growing demand, I started to lose him, physically as well as morally. And with that loss of his presence came the loss of his feelings toward a lot of things. I felt I'd lost his respect, his attention, his value. Yet all the while these public demands became more important than his personal ones, I continued to be there as one of the I-Three and not as his wife. I still felt the situation demanded it. He was not very happy; his toe never healed; there was no time for that.

As usual on tour, we had separate rooms, which at first I had enjoyed. But now, because Bob had the additional responsibility to give interviews and the like, the record company took control of his daily life—when he went to bed, the time he had to wake up, eat, and go. He was on a hectic, more pressured schedule now; when everybody else on the tour was able to rest a little later into the morning after a concert, he had to be up for a 7 A.M. or a 9 A.M. interview. If so-and-so was going to call you from another part of the world, you had to be up to catch their time, even though you had just fallen into bed.

As the lifestyle changed, the women kept coming—the beauty queen or the Miss So and So. Every city we went to, he had to meet the Miss So and So for a photo shoot; it was a part of the promotional thing. "Hello Bob, Queen of the So and So is coming down to the hotel to take pictures with you." And then I would find that she came to take pictures during the day but at night she's there, in the bedroom, and trying to see him again the next night. That made a difference because of his health, which I could not stop my feelings about. I was still concerned about that. All this time the sickness was moving, according to what the doctors later said. The toe grew worse, aggravated by his wearing boots every night for performances. Sometimes we did two shows a night, and then there were the after-show parties. Next night same thing.

I remember one night—I think it was in Paris—that he came back to the hotel with his toe all hurt up, draining, and then the next morning we had to call in the doctor. Along with the doctor came the picture on the front page of the newspaper, of Bob dancing with the beauty queen. I kept saying, "You really didn't have to. After the concert you shouldn't have gone out dancing with your sick toe, or if you're going dancing, wear a slipper." That's when I realized that he wasn't thinking of himself anymore, because self-preservation should come first. As for the one-night stands, the flings, I would say to him, "If you do this you can't do that, because you're weakening one aspect of yourself. And along with the weakness you lose your resistance. The more you can rest is the best for you." And he'd say, "Oh, you're getting jealous now . . . ! Now you're acting like a wife, huh?"

We'd have arguments like that. And people even tried to turn him against me. But then I said to myself, *tschoo,* if I'm gonna be thought badly of, and treated so, then forget it. Because if you don't take care of yourself, then you don't love yourself, Bob, and if you don't love yourself, you can't love me. Because you have to love yourself, don't let other people love you more than you love yourself. That's a mistake. And though some are real fans who love you for your message, others are vampires sucking your blood, your energy, and they're only saying they love you because you're in the *Daily News.*

Then I realized, oh, this is what happens when you finally lose control. I was losing whatever control I'd had, and just as I'd been warned early on, it came with success, with stardom, it came with "I'm too busy for you." And the excuses: "There are things that I have to do, that I *must* do, to be somebody, to make money to send the kids to school. I *have* to work this way." Though I knew Bob was on a mission, he had gotten sidetracked in so many different ways by all the "yes" people—whether he was right or wrong they said yes to him. Still, I said, "We're losing the spiritual aspect of our dreams."

Then there came a time when the whole vibe started to change. This began to happen after Don Taylor had been fired from his job as Bob's manager. Danny Sims, along with Alan Cole, was now managing the tour—Danny Sims, who took our demos over the years and sold them and claimed most of Bob's publishing rights from the early days. And I'm there thinking, wow—what's going on? After Bob had signed with Island, I didn't participate in his financial or managerial decisions.

Then everything began to unravel. At the end of September 1980, we arrived in New York to do a show with the Commodores at Madison Square Garden. The other members of the group were separated from Bob—we were put in the Gramercy Park Hotel downtown, and he was at the Essex House on Central Park South. We had never before been booked into different places like that. I heard later that some hustlers, dreads from Brooklyn who had attached themselves to the tour, had offered him something, though I don't know whether or not he took it.

After the show he'd stayed up all night, Bob told me later. I called him the next morning, which was a Sunday, to ask if he wanted to go to church, because ordinarily whenever we were in a city that had an Ethiopian Orthodox Church, we had been making sure to attend. Pascalene from Gabon answered. When she got on the phone I thought, wow, what's she doing there so early? Then Bob picked up and said he didn't want to go to church, which was unusual, and he didn't sound like himself, so I said, "What happened, you didn't sleep last night?"

He said, "Not really." Then he went on to say that he was fine, but that he couldn't make it to church and he was going to send the limousine for me. Still, something in his voice sounded strange and distant.

Minnie was with me, and I kept having the feeling that something wasn't quite right, so I said to her, "You go up there and see what's happening because I keep having this nagging feeling . . ." All along something just didn't seem right.

When Minnie got uptown and went into Bob's room, she looked at him and—she told me this years later—she saw Death. To her, he looked like a ghost. Eventually they told us what had happened, that Bob collapsed while he was running in Central Park. He and Alan Cole had gone jogging to "energize" Bob, who in mid-run had suddenly felt his body freezing up on him. When he turned to tell Alan that something was wrong, he couldn't move his head or speak, and fell down. Now they were waiting to see Danny Sims's doctor, but Bob wanted us to go ahead to the next concert location, which was Pittsburgh, and he would see us there.

Nobody had said anything to me about Bob falling, which I thought was so disrespectful and suspicious. But then I guess the lifestyle had so broadened, and so many people were riding on our earnings, that he wasn't in control anymore over who knew what or when. Other people had taken over his life completely, and I didn't know—maybe he didn't even know—what he was eating or smoking. I still don't know, though over the years I've heard a lot of stories about what had been going on without my knowledge.

So I did go on to Pittsburgh, even though I knew something wasn't right. During the night I dreamed that Bob was inside a fenced-in place that could have been a hospital, but it had bars and he didn't have any hair on his head. He came to the fence to say something but we were separated by this grill thing, and I woke up thinking again that he didn't look right to me, something had still not been explained. The next morning I called Marcia and Judy and told them about the dream, and then I decided to call New York and see what was happening. When I reached Bob's number there, the phone was answered by a Jamaican journalist named Fitz, who was doing public relations for the tour. When I said, "Fitz, what's happening there?" he said, "Man, it doesn't look right . . ."

I started to panic. "What do you mean it doesn't look right, what the f--- is happening to Bob? What happened to my husband?"

Fitz said again, "Man, something is not right, and they need to talk to you."

At that point I started to curse. "Listen to me!" I said. "If you all stay up there and let anything happen to Bob, you will have to answer questions! Because something is f---ing *wrong*, and nobody's telling me the truth!"

I hung up the phone, and *oh*, I was upset. I began to feel panicky. A couple of hours later, Bob arrived and they said it was time for sound check, so I got on the bus where he was waiting, looking terribly pale. "Bob, what happened?" I said quietly. "Come on man, tell me the truth. You don't look right. What's happen? You didn't sleep? What happened, what happened yesterday?"

He took me aside in the bus, and said, "Well, Danny Sims took me to the doctor, and the doctor says I have cancer."

I felt as if my heart had left my body. I said, "What are you talking about?" I said, "Something is wrong here, somebody's trying to hurt you. Let's go home." Immediately I wanted to go. It was as if I'd gotten so scared that I wanted to stay away from everybody because I didn't know who around was enemy or who was friend.

I jumped off the bus and went to find Marcia and Judy, and told them the story. We were all furious. "Can you imagine this is what Bob is telling me and nobody called us?" Of course everybody was kind of suspicious, but Bob said they were going to do the concert that night anyway.

But I said, "No you don't!" I hunted up Danny Sims and said to him, "How dare you! What is this, a game? How could you do this?"

And then I found Alan Cole. I said, "What *exactly* is happening? Tell me!" And then, finally, they said that the doctor told them that the malignancy in Bob's toe had spread to his brain and that he was going to die anyway, so they might as well continue the tour till he dies.

I was outraged. I said, "No!" And then it seemed as if I needed additional backup, so I ran to the phone and called Bob's mother and told her to please help me out, to please call and intervene. I called Diane Jobson, Chris Blackwell, and Bob's business lawyer, David Steinberg, and told them the same thing. I even called Dr. Bacon in Miami, who said he'd been expecting this and could have prevented it, that things needn't have been this way. I was devastated. Then I ran back to Danny and Alan and screamed, "We can't go on with this, it's crazy! You've got to stop this show now! Now! Stop Stop Stop Stop Stop!!"

. . .

Bob checked into Memorial Sloan-Kettering Cancer Center, where they gave him radiation treatments that resulted in hair loss around his forehead and temples. Cindy Breakspeare came to New York, where she and I shared time caring for him with the kids and Aunty. But word leaked out that he was there, and it got on the radio and in the New York papers, so he left New York for a hospital in Miami, in search of some kind of positive word about treatment or cure. But everyone told him that he had only months to live, that the cancer had advanced into his liver, lungs, and brain and was still spreading. He came back to Sloan-Kettering, where they gave him chemotherapy, and his locks started to fall out, in lumps. He said, "This is dangerous, can it grow back?" And they said, "Oh yes, yadda yadda . . ." He began losing weight rapidly, and it seemed as if he was slowly turning into a different person. The morning of November 4, 1980, he called for a baptism. I'd been telling him to be baptized ever since His Majesty Emperor Haile Selassie sent Abba to Jamaica, because I'd had *all* our children (not only my own) baptized in the Ethiopian Orthodox Church. When he asked me to call Abba that morning, he was crying. We were all crying. Bob was baptized with a new name, Berhane Selassie, meaning "light of the trinity."

A short time after this, Dr. Carlton Fraser, a Jamaican physician who was a Twelve Tribes member, suggested that Bob try Dr. Josef Issels, a German doctor with a specialty in the treatment of advanced cancer. I had gone to Jamaica to check on the children and Aunty and to prepare them for the seriousness of the situation. By the time I was able to leave them, Bob had been taken to a hospital in Germany by Dr. Fraser and Alan Cole. When I called and asked for him, I was told he was having his tonsils taken out. When I asked who—besides me as next of kin—had given permission for that to be done, I was told that the permission had been given by Mr. Alan Cole. My first response was "Why did he do that?" Because I thought that once they touched Bob's tonsils, he'd lose his voice and wouldn't be able to sing again, and that's what they wanted to do.

I got to Germany the day after they removed his tonsils without my knowledge or my approval and found that this was part of Dr. Issels's treatment, that chronically inflamed tonsils and decayed teeth had to be removed if they were getting in the way of the body's natural immune system. Nevertheless I felt—and this was my belief—that operating on Bob's throat was what the Devil wanted to do in the first place, stop his voice from saying what it was saying. I was more suspicious of the whole thing now.

Then I went to see him along with his mother, who had arrived the same day, and he was able to show his happiness on seeing our faces. He was also able to whisper that he'd had a dream about the two of us the night before, and at this he laughed and said, "Now the both of you come." He had dreamed that both of us were drowning and he didn't know which one to save. "Now tell me, Rita," he said, "if you both was drowning, who should I save first, my mother or you?"

Well, I had to laugh and she had to laugh, and I said, "You know you have to save both of us." And then all three of us just began to laugh at the idea, which reassured him that really we would never leave him. I will never forget that morning, because from then on I understood that everything was just going to go downhill.

That same night, when I went back to the hospital, I could see he was very worried. He took my hand and said, "Why you stayed away so long in Jamaica?" Because, even though so many other things were happening, he still looked to me for a certain strength. For him I remained a pillar. When I wasn't around, he felt as if people could do anything they wanted with him, but if Rita was there, she wouldn't allow certain things. She will make an argument of certain things. I was always like that, despite all the women and every other aspect of it. He told me he had told Cindy not to come back to see him again. She had met with Pascalene and knew Bob had been seeing her (it was in the newspaper), and by then Cindy was getting ready to marry someone else and would get married about three months later. So she took herself out of the picture. And soon Pascalene was sent away, too. I guess it didn't feel right anymore, having these women around; I was not comfortable and maybe they weren't either.

From then on, I went back and forth between Germany and Jamaica, bringing some of the things he liked best, things that were healthy like yam and dashine, because Dr. Issels's treatment included the kinds of food that Rastas also thought it proper to be eating. I didn't like other aspects of the treatment—for example, every morning we had to take Bob to Issels's clinic to take pints of blood out, and put blood back in, and I wasn't sure whether Bob was getting back his own blood. Nevertheless, Dr. Issels kept Bob alive more than six months longer than the other doctors had predicted, though he had made no promises other than to try his best. It wasn't until the spring of 1981 that he said he had done all he could, and Bob asked to be flown home. I had gone back to Jamaica when this happened, and he called me to say he wanted to be closer to the children and to his mother and me, that I shouldn't come to Germany, but instead should bring all the children to Miami, where he was going to fly. So he was on the verge but he was determined, and built up that resistance that took him back to Miami, which allowed him to see the kids, and give them instructions, and to tell them that he would always be with them. At one point he called Ziggy and Steve into the room where only the family was allowed. To Steve he said, "Money can't buy life," and to Ziggy, "On your way up, please take me up; and on your way down, don't let me down." And they both said, "Yes, Daddy."

Early on the morning of May 11, from the hospital in Miami, he called Diane Jobson and said to her, "You know, Diane, what will happen if, you know, something happens to me? If I should pass away, as the doctors say, what will happen?" And when she said, "Nothing," he said, "No man, give me a likkle law." He was saying to her, give me the legal aspect of this matter. I swear he said it to her, even in the whisper that was all he could manage. Recently I asked her if she remembered what Bob had said. Because "give me a little law" meant he needed some assurance, since earlier he'd said, "I don't want to write this thing they call will." That morning Diane said, "No, man, your wife and children will be the main beneficiaries, and I'm sure Rita will take care of your mother."

But if she had just said to him "Let me write something and you sign," as his legal adviser at the time, it would have saved millions of dollars. Instead of our having to give away what we didn't have, because when Bob passed away he was not a millionaire, although that's what people think. Of course he knew he had done his work, and what was left to be done was for us to do.

That last day, a little before noon, I had gone to get him some carrot juice and when I returned his eyes were closed and the doctor said, "It's over." I started screaming, "Don't give it up to the Devil, Bob! Give it up to Jah, don't give Satan any power to mingle with your spirit! Don't give up, Bob, don't stop, go straight to your father in Zion high!" I took off the red, black, and green band around my waist and tied it around his head, and kept shouting biblical injunctions until I heard the doctor say, "We better keep her quiet," and the next thing I knew they had given me an injection that put me to sleep. When I woke up Bob was not in the room, and I realized what had happened.

By late afternoon I was still pretty upset, until Steve said to me, "Mommy, you remember what Daddy says, 'No woman no cry.' Daddy says don't cry, no woman no cry. So come, let's go to Jamaica." So Steve and I got on a plane, the last plane leaving Miami at six. And I came straight from the airport to the house on the hill, the house I had taken a chance on before we left on that last tour.

chapter thirteen
WHO CAN BE AGAINST US

B OB'S PASSING WAS a downfall for me. He was my strength, my man, my first heart.

I had never experienced a death in the family since becoming an adult; it was as if part of me went, emotionally and spiritually, even physically—because just the fact that he wasn't there felt strange, to wake up the next day and not be able to look at him. For me, death is not the end of life; I believe the spirit continues and believe in reincarnation in a positive way. But I understood for the first time that sensation of something missing when you lose a person's physical presence.

Bob passed a month after receiving Jamaica's Order of Merit, one of the country's highest honors. I had to bring his remains from Miami to Kingston—we could have taken him anywhere we wanted, but we brought him to Jamaica—which was fitting, at least for the time being, because the most fitting would be Africa, the place he dreamed about and saw himself. And we're looking forward to doing that someday. Let his bones be put in the earth of Africa. That was his dream. But we brought him to Jamaica, for many reasons.

For two days his body lay in state in the National Arena in Kingston. He had one arm over his guitar and a Bible in his other hand. Tens of thousands of people came to pay their respects. There were musical tributes on every street in Kingston. Not only all of Jamaica, but representatives from everywhere in the world turned out for the funeral. The leaders of both political parties spoke; the Wailers played, backed up by the I-Three; and Bob's mother sang, as did a new group of Marleys—Sharon, Cedella, Ziggy, and Stephen, calling themselves the Melody Makers. Then the coffin was driven seventy-five miles to St. Ann and placed in a mausoleum made of local stone.

We, the Marley family, did all the arrangements, with the help of my friends Eleanor Wint, a professor at the university, and Lorna Wainwright, who still works with us. Those were bosom buddies, along with, of course, Minnie and Marcia and Judy. I must mention also the great support we got from Babsy Grange, who later became a Jamaica Labor Party senator. She made sure that Bob had an official grand send-off. So I was fortunate in having friends—sisters—who, when I was unable even to think straight, would say, "Listen man, we've got to do this thing. How? What do you want? What do you want *us* to do, let us . . ." It had to be done, and my friends said, "Oh, don't even think of quitting until certain things are accomplished." Having that help and support was crucial, because with it I was able to get through all the ceremonial, public aspect of the funeral. And Aunty was there, too; she was around for a good time after Bob's death. She lived to see better days.

I felt in the peculiar position of being in the middle of it and aware that it was happening, but floating above it, thinking it just couldn't be. I kept on the denial, on the denial. No no, this is not happening; I'm here but I'm not here. This is not the end. This is all a bad dream kind of thing. I stayed this way for a long time afterward. Bob—he was tired, he was really tired. And I saw him disappear. Yet even now, if people say to me, "When Bob died . . ." and I say, "Bob didn't die," they look at me like, "What?" But I still have that feeling in me, that he didn't die. He's somewhere, I'll see him sometime.

It wasn't until after the funeral that all hell broke loose. I really didn't have time to mourn because I had to go right into meeting with the good, the bad, and the ugly. It wasn't easy, Bob passing without a will or a letter or something.

When I didn't see Peter and Bunny at the funeral, I took note of it— oh, they're not here. Nor did they offer to help, or attend any of the functions. And this blew my mind. At the moment I said to myself, this is unbelievable, although I didn't have time to really focus on them. But after the ceremonies were over and a few months had passed, a lot of things came up, and I'm saying, wow, this is a load I don't think I can carry alone. I'd love to reach out to Bunny and Peter, ask them to participate in this legacy. It wasn't even about money. The assets—music was the main one— were more than money but valueless without proper administration. That would take careful planning, and considering that Bob didn't leave a will, anything could happen.

So I called Bunny and Peter to say that I would love to have a meeting and invited them to come to the Tuff Gong office at 56 Hope Road. I said, "You know it seems only reasonable for you guys to be the ones who come together with me." And I prayed that to myself, even though I knew about the different conflicts and problems that had divided the group in the past. But I put that aside at this point and told myself there was room to start anew, and let this be the line that might reopen the door.

But right away Bunny and Peter arrived with an attitude. First they were hostile to the guard at the gate: "Open this bomboclaat and blah blah . . ." But I took them upstairs to the office. At Hope Road, everything around had to do with Bob—not only the record shop, but photographs, posters from concerts, memorabilia, all that kind of stuff. Suddenly, to my horror, Peter started to pull Bob's pictures off the wall. Pulled down Bob's pictures—and said he didn't want to see no dead man! Unbelievable! Don't want to see no dead man—pull it down! *Eh eh eh bomboclaat!* And Bob not even a year gone, and everybody still mourning!

I couldn't believe this. I hadn't realized the depth of Peter's animosity, the extent of the power struggle, the grievance that was held even to the grave. And Bunny was very much the same, adamant. His position was that Bob's death had been "the wages of his sin and corruption." And I told myself at that very moment that one day I was going to talk about this, because people might need to know. It was not easy to see and hear.

All in the face of my intention to include them, to say "Hey guys, let's continue this work." But they said they were coming in to take over, and they were going to change this and to change that, and they didn't want to see Bob's picture hanging because he was dead. I should close the place down and start anew.

I kept my cool and said I was very surprised at their reaction, though all the while I was thinking, this can't work. Then Bunny said to me—and I have been waiting twenty years for these words to be in print—if *I* would come and work for *them,* give up what I had begun to do . . . I looked at them and could only think, they must be crazy! And then I remembered how bewildered I'd been when I had come into the picture years before. Back then I was so used to women like Aunty and Fat Aunty that I was shocked to discover that to some Jamaican men women were for sex, cooking, washing clothes, having babies, shutting up, and taking licks.

When they were gone I told myself no, no, this is where I put on my armored suit. It's time to fight. Seems like there's gonna be a war here. Bob passed in 1981, and in '82 the war started. By then we'd had to form an estate, and the lawyers would not allow anybody to just come in and do what they wanted. Everything had to be done legally, between the wife and children and the trust, the estate. And if that was Bunny and Peter's attitude and they were planning to come in and take away everything, then neither the children nor I would have anything.

We had a battle, man. *I* had a battle. Those people whom I thought would embrace me and support me just to keep Bob's musical legacy going—I did not know that they were carrying such grudges and wanted only revenge. When I realized this, I said, oh no. I sat down with my family to discuss the situation and they agreed that no, this could not be right. So I had to turn my wheels, and this is when Rita Marley Music came into the picture. I established my own company, and called it RMM—which still means Robert Marley Music, because I'm R and he's R, so it's Rita and Robbie, whatever way you want to look at it.

Sometimes it *hurts,* when you are given caps to wear that you are unprepared for. There was no way I could avoid being the business manager of the Marley legacy, though I didn't really want to be. But I had no choice, there was no one else, and I had to learn on the job, one day at a time. It's quite an experience to do that, to be saying to yourself every day, if I had only known this, or known that, *oh.* But then you try to retain the knowledge: Yes, this is how that goes, now I *know* it.

A lot of people had a lot of thoughts about what should have happened with Bob's estate, especially since I was appointed an administrator. The situation might even have been worse if Bob had made a will and said, "This is for my wife and children," because then I'd have been targeted for *having* it. Instead, I was accused when it was discovered that oh, she doesn't have it, she's *fighting* for it because he didn't leave it to her. Even though I was qualified as his wife, I still had to fight—not only for myself, of course, but for the whole family, since the law states that if a person dies without a will his estate becomes a government's domain, leaving you to show how well or how come you deserve to participate in it.

According to law, the estate had to advertise for anyone who felt that he or she had a claim. Anyone who claimed to be owed anything, or who claimed to be a child of Bob Marley, was given ten days to report. Some of the claims were amazing! There were people much older than Bob who claimed he was their father, others who claimed to have been adopted by me! One guy said he was my aborted child that I thought was dead but had not died. There were people who came to say that Bob had promised to take care of them for the rest of their lives and now they were disappointed that I was not doing that! Things got crazier as the days went by.

There were also big problems with taxes, and so-called friends, and so-called managers. Just before Bob passed, he had called his business lawyer and made him promise to get back all the rights to the early JAD work we had done and give them to his family. That alone became a big problem. Then there were those who "made it happen." So many people "made" Bob that I wondered what Bob had been doing for himself. And they all insisted that "*we* did this and *we* did that." There were so many who tried to take advantage of my situation, to take over a woman who didn't have any experience of this sort. People who were sure that whatever was coming had to be too much for me, all of them looking at material and money.

I felt caught in a trap with everything left blank. The three people who had any clear knowledge of Bob's affairs were Bob's manager Don Taylor (who had been dismissed before Bob passed), his lawyer David Steinberg, and his accountant Marvin Zolt. Those were the people I had to put my head with to really understand what was what and where do we go from here. As I've mentioned, after the JAD days, I was never involved in the business aspect of Bob's career. It was always kept outside of Jamaica, most of it international. Other people took care of the business, because it was enough for me to be in the studio, onstage, or at home with the kids. I didn't start out to be the businessperson that I've become.

I was put on trial—a trial that lasted about six months in the United States—for spending on things that the estate felt did not apply to Mr. Marley. The administrators' complaint was that I had acted illegally, that Don Taylor had told them I was spending millions of dollars, living like a queen, and should be put in jail. He tried to sell me as a young, black, stupid woman whose husband had died leaving her millions—this was the impression he gave people. He misled me, but I knew I had to listen to him nevertheless, because he had actually been handling a lot of Bob's affairs, and he knew a lot. So I had to just stick my head in and hear what was being told, because I had been left stumbling. For a period of time after Bob passed, I had allowed myself to be guided by Don Taylor, although I did not altogether trust him and in the past had often saved his tail from being kicked—by Bob, for being not only unfair but a thief, unable to turn over what he should have. Bob caught Don on cocaine binges many times, on the job yet unable to do his work properly under that influence. And I, foolishly I guess, had always been very sisterly, telling Bob, "Oh oh, poor Don, don't do that, don't do that." Now this was the same Don Taylor who told the estate to put me in prison, because I was spending millions on things that I shouldn't—like taking care of our children, taking care of Bob's mother, doing the things that Bob would have done normally.

It's amazing to me that someone would deliberately prey on a bereaved woman and then turn around and accuse her of the very actions he has led her into. At one point Don Taylor convinced me to buy an apartment in Nassau that he had rented—it would be a good investment and he was broke, he told me. He took me to the place to meet the owners, to the bank to pay for the place. Then he went back to the estate to complain that I had bought a home overseas! All the while, having inside knowledge of Bob's affairs, he knew that there weren't all the millions he told people about. (If Bob had had that much money, he would not have had to work so hard, or so continuously, before he passed.) We have a saying in Jamaica that uses the word "maaga," which means "wretched thin" and applies perfectly to Don Taylor: Sorry for maaga dog, maaga dog turn round and bite you.

The trial was the outcome of a lawsuit against Bob's lawyer and accountant to which the estate joined me, and as a result of which we had to turn around and sue the estate. Actually, we were sued for being creative with what moneys there were and for doing things that were only logical and right and also necessary. I had to buy the property where we are now, the factory on Marcus Garvey Drive, the studio in Jamaica which we're now operating from. I had to prepare the Melody Makers, the Wailers, and the I-Three to go on the road for tours to keep Bob's spirit alive—he had asked Ziggy to do that: "On your way up, take me up." Besides, it was only right—and I *know* Bob would have wanted it—to let the children try this (a tryout that, as anyone can see, has resulted in wonderful things). I had to give the Wailers money and the I-Three money to continue working with Tuff Gong; I had to pay off a lot of debts that they said Bob had left; I had to give Bob's mother money and to finish paying for the house in Miami where she and the rest of her children live, because Bob had a mortgage on it. I had to pay for his funeral. And all these things turned back on me— they wanted to see me go to prison for this.

But everything I did was *legal*. I had been listening to David Steinberg and Marvin Zolt because Bob had always trusted them. I thought that was the right thing to do, to be taking advice from them since he always had, and for doing things he would have done, that they were planning to do with him. I didn't do anything on my own, everything I did was upon recommendations. So I was able to go into court and tell the judge exactly like it was, and I was able to show the judge exactly what *I* did, sir. What difference *I* made when I came into the picture. What difference I made because I *used* this money, and the least was paid upon myself. The judge saw how much promotion I'd done, and how many *more* records I'd caused to be sold, and the jury knew I'd only tried to do right—how can you steal from yourself?

I have the transcript of the whole thing. It was deep, but we won and, funnily enough, all the complainants, including Don Taylor, are now dead.

Another trial that I had to endure after Bob's passing was the one in which Danny Sims sued us for the rights to the catalogue that Bob owned.

In defense of Danny Sims's position, his lawyer called people who testified that Bob's songs belonged to Danny! This ordeal seems perfectly to illustrate Bob's song in which he says, "your best friend can be your worst enemy and your worst enemy your best friend." I was on tour during that period of the trial, which took place in a Manhattan court. At one point we were playing Manhattan, and as I didn't think I should show my face in the courtroom, I asked a member of my entourage—my chef Obediah— to pass by and just see what was going on. As it happened, he entered the courtroom just in time to hear Don Taylor telling the judge how Bob Marley had been one of Jamaica's most dangerous men! When Don noticed him, he told the judge that I had sent Obediah to kill him—and asked to have Obediah removed!

All the while, throughout these trials and tribulations, I'm saying I know I didn't do anything wrong. Because I was only trying to help a man who went too soon—who brought light to my life and who had helped me, in many ways, when I was young.

I want to make that perfectly clear! I thought Bob did the greatest thing by leading me to find myself. Yes! Who else could I have given myself to? If I'd have gone on to another man, I might have become someone else. But then I was obedient to him, because what he said was so important. "You are what you are, you are black and you are beautiful." And I know there are many, many others who learned that same lesson from him.

It's still not easy, but it's a little easier now because the kids are taking up some of the fight, as well as the responsibility: "This is what my daddy did, this is not what he meant, this is what he didn't do, but this is what he wanted to do." So we have had to consider certain things. We lost a lot of money that we could have had. But that's Bob. He wasn't as interested in making money as he was in getting his message and his music across the world. Being able to go to Italy and outdo the pope in numbers of attendance—that meant more than a million bucks to him!

For the past twenty years my focus has been Bob's business and Bob's music, which I'm saying not to take praises but to explain that if someone hadn't been there to see to it, this legacy might have died. In 1984 I suggested to Chris Blackwell, "Let's just continue Bob's work, let's put the Wailers to work, put the I-Three to work. Give them support and we'll go out and we'll campaign Bob Marley music."

Chris said, "That's not necessary, because Bob is over, and in another two years his music is not going to be sold as much, so there's no need to spend money on a tour."

I said, "Chris, you're crazy. Not while we're alive. Because we were part of that time; Bob didn't work alone. He had our support and we are still here as his support, and I feel that we should carry on, that we *can*, that we *must* carry on." And we did set off with the "Legend" tour.

At that point my focus was around maintenance. How do I keep Bob's momentum, keep the respect people have for him, keep his music alive, keep the pathway for his kids to follow—and at the same time not be offensive, not deliberately overexpose myself, my personal feelings, my personal *wants*. Because it was not—ever—about me. I tried, and I think I was able, to turn my career down for a while. Because even though we knew Bob had done a lot of work, there were still things he could achieve, honors that might come to him that were not given while he was alive. And it was our job—and that of his fans—to make sure those were given. Getting into the Rock and Roll Hall of Fame, for example, a significant achievement only gained after his passing—we had to make that happen by continuing to keep his legacy working. And it happened through the love of his old fans as well as the new ones who never had a chance to see him alive but were loving his music just the same.

Often it was more of a great task than a happy one, a great overwhelming responsibility. One that by its very public nature frightened Aunty—dear Aunty, who had stood by me all this time—until she was saying things like, "They're gonna kill you" and "Please, don't have a boyfriend." As if the course of my life was now to be determined by other people. But I said, oh no, I can't let that happen, I can't let other people rule my actions. I saw Bob lose himself to people and learned a lesson, and I'm not giving anyone that privilege. I mustn't forget Rita, because I saw I was in danger of losing Rita. This wasn't about Bob now, this was about other people trying to use me through Bob's channel. And I'm saying, oh, if I give myself to this, I won't have any of *me* left *for* me. I've got to save myself so that I can bring up my children, because these were *my* children now, and still so young—in 1985 Sharon was nineteen, and then like stair steps were Cedella, Ziggy, Stephen, on down to Stephanie, who was eleven—and psychologically they had been through much more than most children their age. (It's not easy sometimes, being the children of a celebrity.) So I had to double up on myself, to stay strong against use and abuse. I had to sometimes remind myself that I'd been to school, that I'd been trained for this. There were things I would excuse Bob for because he didn't get the training, but I knew enough to defend my rights.

Still, I have not been in this alone. I've had good lawyers and accountants, a good staff and supporters, loyal to me as they had been to Bob. I've had friends who have stood by me and helped to make certain decisions. And I've had my faith.

In the year 2000, *Time* magazine awarded the title "Song of the Century" to Bob's song "One Love" and the title "Album of the Century" to our album *Exodus*. These honors, for which Bob worked so hard, were given to him by qualified people who treated his music with the dignity it deserved and ensured him a proper place in musical history.

When I thought about keeping Bob's memory and his work alive, the first thing that came to mind was to do something educational with the property at 56 Hope Road. This resulted in some controversy, because his mother wanted to keep it as a house she could come to and bring friends and family. But, after a meeting, a decision was made that we all agreed to, and the property became the Bob Marley Museum. I just felt he would have depended on me to do that. Then, too, I thought of the millions of people who were sharing his inspiration, which was so special. And I thought they would like to come and see where some of this music history happened.

As I've mentioned, when Bob first began to use the place, Tuff Gong had to contend with the fact of its location. Not only was it a block away from the prime minister's office, it was also near King's House, where the Queen of England stays when she visits. The complaints that started then—"You can't create such a thing on a road like this, and why are you doing it?"—were now directed at me: "Rita Marley is crazy, makin' a shantytown scene in the uptown area!" But now we are able to fly our Rasta flag, and the flag of Jamaica flies also, along with flags from other countries. Bob himself wouldn't have done that, he wouldn't have thought it would be *allowed*. I can hear him saying it: "Rita, how could you do that, it's not *allowed!* You *crazy?*"

But some crucial things have changed in Jamaica, as in the rest of the world, since the 1970s. Back then, you'd never have seen a picture of Bob Marley on a billboard, or people with dreadlocks advertising Coca-Cola. If Bob had not been successful with them, if he hadn't earned victory wearing that crown of the Rastaman, things wouldn't be the same. Though certainly today the whole idea is different—you don't have to read your Bible to wear locks. We had to read a chapter a day, and had to know *why* we were on this pathway. But now you can go to the hairdresser, sit in the chair, and come out looking like—you're locked, you're born this way, you're made this way! Look at that! It seems a long way from the days when I was accused, abused, scorned, disrespected, even spit on. ("Look at she!—all the education her Aunty tried to give her and now look at she!")

Fifty-six Hope Road remains almost the same structure it was when Chris Blackwell bought it and gave it to Bob. It's an old wooden house that has largely retained its look through our efforts to preserve it; some of the original wood is still around and some has been restored to keep the flavor. The museum is operated by the Bob Marley Foundation, a charitable organization, and hundreds of thousands of people from all over the world have visited. Over the years we've added different features, thanks especially to Neville Garrick, who has given us a lot of inspiration and much of his time to the upkeep of the project. Apart from the historical artifacts, writings, and photographs, there's now an Exhibition Hall and an eighty-seat theater. There are guided tours and videos of Bob's live concert performances. Different clips on Bob's life as well as other features are shown at the end of each tour.

The Marley family members are all part of the place in different ways. It's always amazing when visitors see a member of the family on the grounds and rush to you for autographs, which we always pleasantly give. We have a gift shop and a boutique with African arts and crafts—Stephanie runs that—and recently we've added a little shop called "Bob's Cream," where we sell ice cream and other natural snacks. The Queen of Sheba Restaurant, which still functions as an integral part of the museum, serves fruit drinks and natural foods. We are able to get our seasonings directly from Ethiopia, and we serve *doro wat*, vegetables, stews, wine made from honey (called *teg*), and other things that you would get in an Ethiopian restaurant. And we burn Ethiopian incense there, so that when you walk in you feel like you're on Ethiopian ground. We try to make it as authentic as possible. Our tables are made from Ethiopian straw, our stools are Ethiopian, and we're trying to speak Amharic—*tenalistilin* means hello!

At Universal Studios in Orlando, Florida, there's now a section called the Bob Marley Tribute to Freedom, where a lot of our history can be seen, artifacts and memorabilia we've given to them. This is also our doing, in order to keep spreading the message and music of Bob Marley, another venture for which Chris Blackwell had to give his approval (Chris still helps with certain decisions about Bob). "Bob doesn't need that, Bob is already high in the sky," he said. But my position was, whatever can take him higher . . . Oh, I had a hard time with that one, but I just felt it was something that was going to make Bob even bigger, which is exactly what has happened. We have concerts there every February 6, for his birthday, featuring some of our children, Ziggy Marley and the Melody Makers, Kymani, Damian, and Julien Marley, myself, the I-Three. There's a lot of punch still happening, and we have made it so there's no gap. Bob keeps coming in from the cold, and I'm happy to be a part of that, and satisfied that we've done so well in maintaining his work. As he said, "Dem a go tired fe see me face, can't get me out the race . . ."

As for me, it's not just about being his wife, it's about being a person who is carrying on a legacy that means so much to the world. Because not only do people my age remain interested, but newer generations, a third and fourth generation, all come loving his message and still wearing his T-shirts and singing his songs at concerts.

chapter fourteen
THE BEAUTY OF GOD'S PLAN

I F I GO back to every page in my life, almost every significant moment was something I hadn't planned for or didn't expect to happen. Because sometimes I ask myself, how did I get into this? *Why* did I get into this? Why *me?* When I analyze it all, I see that events didn't happen for the sake of themselves, or only for the day they happened, but to propel a whole series of events, for a particular time to begin, for more purpose to be added. As for what I did to make this happen—I simply decided to live a certain way. Now, what I appreciate most about the life I chose is that the past hasn't disappeared but is reflected in and flows into the present, and this seems important. Often I say to young people, I didn't know a Rita Marley when I was like you, though sometimes I wish I had. But maybe I was just supposed to be the one to figure certain things out.

Today I see this push toward independence becoming more common. In nearly every household—black, white, whatever—there's one child with an intention to be conscious, to choose change: "Well my parents were that, but *I* am . . . I have decided to be this, or try that, or do this."

I guess it goes back to the idea I kept hold of, that Rita meant something, Rita came for a purpose, Rita had a life to live. Plus Rita now has children, and she's living to be here for them. And I'm living to see my grandchildren, too. Thirty-eight so far! Of course I didn't do it alone, there are other mothers. But then *raising* them . . .

They were always treated as normal children and taught to expect no more or less than their friends and classmates. Still, in school or other public places they were faced with who they were, and so they were admired as the superstar's children and criticized as Rastafarians. Limiting as those definitions might be, the kids dealt with them. When necessary, they fought to be considered on their own merits. The worst for them, I know, was being without Daddy after his passing, because he was the fun father who always loved, always provided. He loved to be there for them, and had been getting ready to do just that.

The Melody Makers took their name from a British rock magazine, *Melody Maker*, after they happened to see a poster for an issue with a cover story about Bob Marley and the Wailers. Their first single, issued in 1979, was *Children Playing in the Streets*. The title comes from the only song Bob lived to write for them. At one point Stephanie and Karen, their little sisters, "managed" the group, when they weren't yet professional, and everybody was still going to school. Though not among the singers and the youngest of them all, they would always be at the rehearsals, always mixed into everything and telling the older ones what to do.

When the Melody Makers finished school and began professional musical careers that included touring, I felt I had to travel with them. They needed my support. Even if they were old enough to perform professionally, I felt I had to be chaperone and manager, to be able to say, when they started out, "Mommy's here." They were signed to EMI, and then went from EMI to Virgin and then to Electra. Nothing I did for them felt strange or burdensome, although I suppose you could say I went from background vocalist to backstage mother. But I have no regrets. I don't ever think about what I might have missed out on—actually, it doesn't seem like I've missed anything. Because I was able to guide them, they didn't have to go out there and come back saying, "Oh, we had a bad experience." For me, it was easy to sort out the good and the bad, and to show them this kind of good, that kind of bad. "This is how we do it, this is how Daddy would do it, this is how we'd do it when Daddy was going." My being there made it all easier for them to understand. And they became winners! Four-time Grammy winners, and in the Top Ten of reggae entertainers. Whatever time and sacrifice on my part were certainly for good reasons, yes! And I still feel that way.

Of course, when I started to ease out and to think about going back to my own career, I would hear: "Mommy, you're not coming on tour? Mommy, you can't do that!" In defense I had people actually trained on the road with them—Addis Gessesse and his brothers from Ethiopia, who are still with us—and then eventually I said, "You know what, I'm gonna leave you, and you'll work next year by yourself."

Naturally their response was, "We can't manage, they won't listen to us!" But indeed they have managed, and very well. The best thing about these kids is that they're so—what should I call them? Not only obedient, but they're kids without any airs. They don't have attitudes, I guess you might say. They're just open. And friendly. Very natural, down to earth. They don't feel that because their Daddy is so and so, then they must be so. No, they were taught to be themselves. And they were taught at an early age, humility is the first policy. And manners. Those things. We don't have money, but we're going to have good manners. Just that alone—if you say good morning, and thank you, you make a good impression. When they were in that teenage stage, you never found them in some of the situations other kids often get into because of inexperience. Not many problems back then, and now they are grown, with children of their own, and they haven't forgotten what they were taught.

During all the tears and trials after Bob passed, I would get home from work and find that I was still bugged. I felt as if I were becoming hard as a rock from all the abuse, from being continually accused and chastised, as if darts were being thrown at me. I was losing my natural self, my smile. I remember even doing a song with the lyric "My smile has gone away." It took a while before I finally woke up to the fact that I was still alive and well. Though the children and I were able to manage without a father at home, there were times we did need a man to *be* there, just to take up some of the responsibility that it takes to make a family. Or just to help *me*— because there were times when I thought nobody was thinking about *me*— it was still all about Bob. And I needed those moments when someone would think about me. And love me!

When I opened my eyes, I didn't have far to look because I had an old friend, Owen Stewart, my good friend Tacky, who still cared for and checked on me. Between us we always had more than just sex, but love and caring. So I was able to open my heart, and we redeveloped our relation-ship. Because the kids knew him and were familiar with him as "Mommy's friend," it wasn't as if I were bringing anyone new into their lives. And Tacky, as always, was a real friend, who supported me and gave me encour-agement and strength not to pay the backbiters any mind. "Worry less and work less," he always said, and "take a rest."

Serita, my last daughter, is Tacky's child, and came almost when every-thing was about to be over, I thought. So as we say in Jamaica she was the "washbelly," my final child. And that was it—that *is* it! Serita and I became very close because of my having had her after all the other kids were quite grown—after having five and it seemed as if I surely wasn't going to have any others (although I know if Bob had still been around, we would have had a few more). But Serita came at a time when, *ooh*, I needed this. I needed something to slow me down from the hustle and the hassle, often from 9 A.M. to 10 P.M. Those nine months I really had time to relax— it was just me and the baby in my belly. And that was very good for a change, even though I still had to go to work. The other kids cherished those moments of seeing me pregnant and were thrilled at the prospect of a new baby in the family—the house needed that. Still, some asked, "Why?" Like Aunty. When I told her the news, she said, "Oh, no, what people are gonna say?" Even though this was five years after Bob's passing, she said, "Oh, you shouldn't have a baby, because people are gonna say this and say that . . ."

I said, "Aunty, stop! To hell with other people, this is *my* life! Besides, I didn't do this alone, someone else was involved! And if God wants it so, it makes me happy."

Even today, Serita is still my "purse," as I call her, a name she acquired because I had to take her on tour—three months after she was born we had to hit the road. To help with her I took along Minnie's mother, whose name is Rita Mazza and whom we called "Miss Rita." Serita is Serita Mazza, and I'm Rita, so we had a Triple Rita thing going. As a baby Serita would give Miss Rita trouble sometimes—poor Miss Rita, though she never complained, keeping up with Serita was fun, but on the road it could be hard work!

After my father came back to Jamaica for Bob's funeral, he decided to stay. He was getting older and realized the importance of just being around us. By then Wesley was in Canada with his family, as was my brother Donovan, who had been raised by our mother. Papa's other children, including Miss Alma's Margaret and George and our Swedish sisters, had branched out, too.

So Papa came home, where he graduated to "Pops." When Pops assessed the responsibilities he might assume in the family business, he decided to make himself available musically for a session every now and then and to take over the maintenance department of Tuff Gong. His carpentry experience proved to be invaluable. He maintained chairs and desks and windows and doors, fixed leaks and anything else that needed attention. And oh, everyone loved Pops, he was a big favorite and very very helpful. He would say, "Rita, I'm watchin' your back, you know." And sometimes he'd call me in the evenings to fill me in on my staffing problems. He'd say, "Listen man, this guy jokin', he's not doin' a hundred percent, he's jokin'!" That was Pops, watching my back. In his last days, Pops was there for everything.

And Aunty was there for her baby brother. Naturally, as big sister (small as she was), she maintained her usual bossy attitude, and at first there was a little rivalry going. Because Pops thought, why is she still running everything? He was astonished to find when he came back that Aunty continued to be in charge! Even after all these years and responsibilities, and grandchildren and all of that! Pops worried a bit that she still didn't allow me to make my own decisions. But I was grateful to her by then, and knew what to allow and what not to. And I felt that her continuing abilities freed me to do more for myself.

The competition between Pops and Aunty was sorted out when they each got their own apartment and became neighbors on Washington Drive, in the three-sister house where I had once lived. As always, though, Aunty made her daily trips up the hill to be sure everything was okay. She had a car then, and a driver, the same person who took the kids to school. Oh, she had to be in that car to make sure they got to school and make sure they went safely into their classrooms on time. And when school was over, the driver would have to pick her up first to go pick them up—she never gave anybody else a chance!

Dear Aunty. Eventually I made sure that she had everything she had ever wanted, though at one point she was determined to drive. I kept saying, "No—you have a car and a driver, why must you drive?" But she was insistent that she didn't want this person, Mr. Andy, who the hell he thinks he is, she's gonna drive herself! And one day I was amazed to see her, barely visible behind the wheel, coming up the hill! I could not believe my eyes, I went crazy, I almost sacked the driver. I said, "How dare you let her drive!"

And the poor man said, "But Mrs. Marley, I couldn't stop her! Because if Aunty feels she can do it, she's gonna do it!"

And she did fine—she drove herself home down our winding mountain road and subsequently announced to me, "I can take the kids to school now!" She was just irrepressible, yes, that's the word for her. Even though age was coming and she wasn't able to do her dressmaking anymore, she still would advise me about my costumes: not to wear this or that, or how something should be made, and how she would do it in the days when she was sewing. And she always won.

Aunty was the next of my family to pass away, taking another, large piece of me with her. But when she went to rest, she did it gracefully and peacefully. The doctor called us one morning to say that she had gone to sleep the night before and never woke up. She hadn't been feeling well but wasn't particularly sick. I was five months pregnant with Serita, and I remember screaming my heart out till I thought I was going to have the baby right then. We rushed to the hospital, where Aunty was lying in bed as if she were fast asleep; Cedella even tried to give her mouth-to-mouth resuscitation. But that didn't work, so we brushed her hair and told her good-bye. That was very very hard on me, losing my *tootoos,* my Vie Vie. But surely she must rest in peace, because so many people loved her.

Steve had been her pet, and the night before she died she told him how she'd been feeling lately. "Aunty said she don't mind if she die now," he told us afterward, "because she can't take the politics, the pressures that you are having with people, everybody coming at you, wanting this thing or that thing Daddy left, wanting money . . ." She thought, Steve said, that if she died she'd look over us better, protect us more, she was getting too old to keep up.

Poor Aunty, I thought. Marley wasn't an easy name to carry or be associated with during those times, though there were always good and bad sides and the situation subsequently improved. When, in the late nineties, I was awarded Jamaica's Order of Distinction, I remember thinking, oh Aunty should be here to see this, this is what she would go crazy over, something is happening where the *government* is involved! But I know she's around in spirit, working her wings off.

She didn't live to see Serita born, but Serita looks a lot like her, and all the others knew her for all their growing-up years. They remember how Aunty and her pal Miss Collins would sit with them evenings and fold their socks. With five kids (it grew to ten sometimes) and each with a few pairs, you can imagine the task. But that was Viola Anderson Britton. They don't come like her every day. She was, as we would say, a sample. And I was lucky to have her for as long as I did.

I guess it was because I felt so lucky to have had Aunty, and was so aware of the importance of family guidance, that I felt I really had to care for Bob, because I thought there was something he lacked when growing up that he was trying to catch up with—that mother time which is so important. The effect a mother has on her son. Plus, when you hear "like father like son," and you don't have a father around, you try to cling even more to what Mommy or Grandma has to offer. But sometimes Mommy has to leave, and often not because she wants to. Who can blame any mother, stuck there in Trench Town with kids. Bob's mother didn't want to end up a nobody, so as a young striving girl she had to escape. I can imagine her thinking, what am I supposed to do? And there she had her son and a little baby. In this situation poor Bob became a victim, losing that period when he still needed his mother's protection but instead had to be on his own, earning his keep by tying up goats and working for this one and that one. But Mommy was a victim too, had to go fight life to find a life. So if you go back and look into her life, mine is like . . . the next step.

Not long after Aunty went to rest, my father passed. I was so bereft I kept thinking, where do I turn now? I thought I could never live without Pops and Aunty. How would I make it without their love and support? But I lived through the losses and learned to lean on my friends more and treasure their advice. Dahima, an American, turned out to be one of the best sisters I ever had. Bob had met her in California on one of our tours—she was working for Margaret Nash in Los Angeles—and I think they started out as "friends." She moved to Jamaica with her children after he invited her to come and work for him, but when she and I were introduced she made it clear that she'd found out it wasn't going to be what she thought it would be. (She hadn't known Bob was married to me until she came to Jamaica and saw my family.) Nevertheless, she stayed in Jamaica and raised her kids for a period of time here, and we became good friends. It was Dahima who got me started wearing lipstick. One day she said, "Girl, you've got those sexy lips, use them!"

I said, "Are you crazy? No, Bob would kill me!"

"No, Rita," she said, "all you have to do is add a little vitamin E oil. I'll bring you some from America, and you must use it! It'll bring out your beautiful smile!"

I progressed from vitamin E oil to lip gloss to color. And I've really enjoyed it ever since. After Bob's passing, Dahima thought I was being abused and stayed by my side to encourage me and help me to carry on. She was skilled in the publishing aspect of the music business and was especially supportive of my business ability and had a way of making me feel special. "Listen, girl," she'd say, "you can do it. Let's form a company." So I believe she, too, took her sour and made lemonade. For a woman, inner strength and self-reliance are all-important: You really have to be the best driver at the wheel, especially when you're steering and changing gears at the same time. Just make sure you don't have a head-on collision!

In Jamaica, where violence can rear up at any time, I've learned to be especially careful. I've had the wackiest things happen. Recently a guy came to my office to say he was the reincarnated Bob and that he needed to see me, and then walked the road several times, watching my vehicle go up and down. I've been stalked by people who have a vision that I belong to them. People sneak! I've had to put up extra security gates because they would lie in wait for me on the road, just to see me driving from the museum back to my house. But Jamaica is a place where you're loved today and hated tomorrow. It's one thing being Rita Marley but another thing being a Rasta. People like me for being Rita, but then they turn around and dislike me for being a Rasta.

These days, everyone tries to copy what we were promoting back then as the Rasta lifestyle—vegetarianism, organic food, exercise. I suppose that does, or doesn't, include the smoking of herb. As we see it, it's a God-made plant, just like all the other herbs in the garden. And there are of course the much-publicized medical uses—for glaucoma and pain relief. As for me, I've always used marijuana as a sacramental food. Whenever I've felt as if I wanted to do the right thing the right way, or say the right thing at the right time, I have a puff or a cup of tea. It's good for my meditation, it has its use, but of course anything that you overdo can be harmful. I prefer to use it as just another plant from the garden that has its good purposes, and go for the good purposes.

When I looked into myself to try to separate needs from wants, to come to terms with the next stage of my life, I realized soon enough that I had enough material stuff, that I could do something besides have more. If at a certain point in your life you have all you need, it's time for you to figure out what's important. What else can you do? If now you're able to give, then it's time to pass on something. As I've said, it was always our way to be giving. This idea has guided me into the next part of my life, by leading me to Africa, where I now spend part of my time in a mountain village, helping the people who live there in whatever way I can. Africa has come like a new life to me, with an ancient background, because it's so black; and because of this I feel at home—that fight you face against your blackness in other places does not exist there. I want the freedom to be what I am, and what I'm supposed to be, without having to fight anybody to be that.

I feel free to embark on this life because the kids are now mature and standing on their own two feet. They know where we're coming from and where we're going today. Going to Africa was part of Bob's philosophy, too—his dream, it wasn't mine alone. So even though he's not here physically, his physical *share* is making sense, filling others' needs because ours have been fulfilled.

chapter fifteen
SUNSHINE AFTER RAIN

M Y FIRST TRIP to Africa was with Bob, to celebrate Zimbabwe's
independence. Then we went to Gabon, where he met Pascalene.
After Bob passed, I traveled to Ethiopia, which for me was very special, a
dream come true, like putting a foot in heaven's door. I was even able to
leave a piece of his locks there. But when it came time for me to find a place
to settle in Africa, where I might have a home and a purpose, Ghana was
the country that opened its heart and its arms. Its stable government was
attractive, as well as its embrace of development. The Rita Marley Foundation was registered there as a nongovernmental organization in the year
2000. Though having that sanction makes things easier, we had begun giving there some years before. Caring for infants and protecting the aged are
our main goals.

I believe that nothing happens by accident. When someone or something is in the right place at the right time, the answers to your questions
come alive. My concern for Ghana came about when I went to look at
a house that I eventually bought near a village called Konkonuru, in the

mountains of Aburi, outside the capital city of Accra. I guess I could have chosen to live anywhere, but I liked the people in that area and those soft mountains, which reminded me of Jamaica. The track that led to this house passed by the village school and reminded me of Trench Town, and as I drove past, I noticed the children sitting on the dirt floor. They had no desks, no seats; the teacher had a chair and a little table. The image stuck in my mind. Years and years ago, trying to follow in Aunty's footsteps, I used to teach in a Sunday school next door to our house in Trench Town, and of course I've always been interested not only in religious instruction from the Bible but in the value of education in general. In Ghana, I went back and forth a few more times to see this house, and each time those children were right in front of me with eyes like angels. Because I didn't *have* to live in that particular location and situation, I realized that my being there must have been for a reason, and now I could see it. After I put down a deposit on the house I got in touch with the headmaster of the school, and the village chief, and the next time I arrived there I had benches for the school with me. Not long afterward, we were pulling down windows and doors from a building in Jamaica and I kept flashing on the school in Konkonuru, which was completely without such amenities. So I found myself calling my secretary to say, "Get me a shipping container, I'm gonna take all that lumber and whatever else is useful from that building to Africa."

She said, "But Mrs. Marley . . ."

I said, "No 'buts,' let's do it!" I just knew that it had to be done. And it was a blessing! Every time I pass by the school it just thrills me to see those doors and windows, because I think, wow, look at that, all this wood was almost burned in Jamaica or thrown away, and here it is keeping out drafts and dew from the classrooms. So this is what we—and when I say "we" I'm talking about my family and friends—are doing. (I remember Dahima pulling down a shack over a hole that was all they had for a toilet; we corrected that.) We don't think there's any "contentment." Yes, we're living a certain way that we can afford to, we're driving cars, and all that. But there's never a moment that we forget the people who can't. And how we can help, not just by giving but by teaching.

I still love to shop, although I've stopped doing that so much now, because I can't build a big enough closet! Whenever I can't find anything to wear because I have too many clothes, I pack barrels to send to Ghana and Ethiopia. In the village we give away some and put others in a thrift store so people can learn to be self-sufficient. We show them how this can work: You get donations, then sell things and use the money for school lunches. Because our purpose isn't all about giving, it's about achievement and self-sufficiency. Recently I had a letter of thanks from the headmaster of the school, who informed me that the bus we had donated is being used as transport from the village into the city, as a way of earning money so they can take care of their own expenses. It's very satisfying to know that not only money but knowledge is being given. To me that's most important. Because coming from zero and being able to own a thirty-seat bus, something must have happened, and you didn't win the Lotto? Then you must have worked extremely hard and you must have had some kind of ambition. Which is a very good example to provide.

Recently Cedella had a barrel of stuff from her "Catch a Fire" clothing collection after the season changed. When she said, "Mommy, take this to your people in Ghana," I was thrilled. And then she looked at me and said, "Mommy, don't *sell* them, *give* them away, please." I guess she knows her Mommy likes to recycle!

I suppose a lot of people wouldn't do all this; maybe they'd just build another house for themselves, or buy another diamond. I've seen people do that. Well, diamonds and pearls are great, but I've never seen myself buying them. Wealth and fame are things that I see as *added*, not given. What is given is life, and for whatever is added, give thanks. If sometimes it seems as if more is added, I give more. And then it seems as if when you give, you get. It's a blessing when you find that you're allowed to make other people happy in whatever way you can. And I have a feeling that just by doing good I've grown to understand the *value* of doing good.

For example, every year since Bob went to rest, when his birthday comes around we do things, organize events in his honor or some such, not only in Jamaica and Ghana but elsewhere if possible. I get excited, and his presence seems everywhere again. I'm very sure why I'm doing this after more than twenty years, because something spectacular invariably happens shortly afterward, like I'll get something in the mail or a phone call that really makes me feel terrific.

Something else we're doing up there in the mountains of Aburi is building a recording studio, which will also house a radio station, where professional engineers will be available to train young people who have the talent and ambition to work in the field of music. (There's a lot of music in Ghana; it feels like a music capital that hasn't been touched.) A studio like this—another of our dreams come true—will provide sound for movies, videos, overdubs, sound effects, and much more, adding to the development Africa so needs. We will also offer accommodations and food from our organic farm, right there in the mountains, where the air is fresh and clean!

All these ideas about giving to Africa simply follow what we have been doing in Jamaica. Bob set the pace, because giving was his style. But then he would give money, mainly, and we realized, no, that's not the best sometimes; you give money and it's done and the same person comes back to you as if you've never given to them. So the Bob Marley Foundation in Jamaica went after other things: We've helped families to start businesses, for example, small enterprises such as cold supper shops like the one Aunty ran for a while in Trench Town. We've adopted orphans. We also give equipment and medicines, donated by other charities, to the Children's Hospital; we help support the Maxfield Park Children's Home; and we've brought doctors into Jamaica just to check on sick people. We found doctors who volunteered their services; Ziggy brought them in through the Melody Makers' organization URGE.

The Melody Makers also have a foundation. Adidas sometimes supports their tour and gives them boxes of shoes and sports gear, which they give away. Sometimes I see things I like, that I would wear, but it's hard for me to get even a pair of sneakers! "Oh, no, Mommy, just tell us, we'll buy you some because these are for the needy!" They give every one away!

In Jamaica, however, when you give too much you become a threat to the system, which is something I've experienced. Maybe that really motivated my turning toward Africa, because once you're a giver, you're always going to want to give, even when you find that what you're giving can be held against you, and that you have to be careful how you give and who you give to.

It's a concern, and you always have to have it in the back of your mind—although given my history, I have to put it up front. I'm forced to keep my guard up, to keep my grit up, spiritually and physically. Be prepared. It's important, especially as a black woman. As Bob said in one of his songs—and he said this years ago!—"You give your more to receive your less/now think about that." I remember saying to him, "Why do you say that?" What I'm realizing as life and time reveal themselves is that Bob Marley's words fall into place. I often find myself saying, "Oh, that's what he felt (or meant)," or "Oh, that's what he saw coming." Because of his advanced political sense, and his being able to sing about what he couldn't even talk about, a lot of people think of him as a prophet. Of course some people dismiss the idea—"Oh a prophet!" They're thinking of an Old Testament god with long white hair and flowing robes. But Bob was just tuned into the reality of the system, and how it needed to change to strengthen the weak. He was simply prophetic—he didn't have to wear a robe. Anyway, all he ever wanted to wear was his old blue work shirt, his jeans, and the boots he loved.

· · ·

Sometimes you're pulled into your past, and you want to go back to the streets you ran as a child. Every once in a while I drive over to Greenwich Park Road and reminisce. When I was a child, a local madman would often write on the part of the cemetery wall facing our house. One day he wrote "Black Police Brutality," and those words are still there! To find where my house was—because the houses and fences are different, in fact the whole landscape is different now—I just look for that graffiti, and when I see it I know I'm in the right place. But my plum tree is gone from the yard where we used to sing and tell stories, and so are a lot of people we grew up with and worked with in Trench Town. As Bob sings, "Good friends we've had/good friends we've lost/along the way." Tata's kitchen, on Second Street, where Bob used to sleep, is being restored so that it can be used as an exhibition center; the Jamaica Tourist Board has invested money in it to try to capture the moment of Bob Marley's time in Trench Town. (I like to go there to visit the spot where Bob and I first made love.) But I was told recently that visitors have been discouraged from going there because of the violence.

Still, each time I want to remember—or make sure I never forget—I go and stand next to the wall that says Black Police Brutality. Back then, young men sitting on the sidewalk would have to get up and run when they saw a police car coming, whether they were thieves or not. We didn't see white people being hit by batons and being threatened: "Get out, get out, get out of the road!" And it wasn't white but black police who were brutalizing black people. You can imagine the madman picking up on all this and just putting it on the wall. I first saw it when I was ten, I'm fifty-six now and it's still there. And what it says is still going on. If anything, there's even more brutality than ever within the area.

Can anything good come out of Trench Town? That was always the big question. Of course I did, as did many more like me. But one recent morning I heard a Jamaican politician on the radio, speaking about how the people in power must realize that Trench Town is still there and still in trouble.

Though the standard of living has risen, and people there are better off these days than we were in the fifties, with nicer houses, cars, and clothing, the reality is that living in certain areas you're still in trouble after all these years, still targeted by the police, and still in a place where brutality exists, just as it did when Bob wrote "Concrete Jungle" and "Them Belly Full (But We Hungry)." Jamaican society remains set up as it was.

Everyone knows that education is the key to a peaceful, productive society, yet a family still must pay to educate its children beyond the primary grades, after about age twelve, unless each child gets a full scholarship. Even with the benefit of a half scholarship, as I was given, my brother had to leave college so that I could go to high school. You have to be in high school by thirteen or you're looked down upon, which means there's no question of "saving up" for school. You have to be clean, your shoes have to shine, and you still have to buy your books and your lunch and your uniforms. Suppose you can't afford these things? Where do you turn? People come to the Bob Marley Foundation with long lists of books their children need. We run a program that lends books: We get them and give them to students and when they finish with them we collect them and give them to others. We see this as a duty to help support families and students; still, there are many more people who remain not only out of our reach but out of the reach of others who could help.

In my opinion, women leaders are what a country like Jamaica needs. That's the only change that might make any difference. Over the years it seems each time elections come around, the political situation explodes into violence, and poor people start killing off one another in the rural and city ghetto areas. It doesn't change; you never hear of them killing one of the ministers for not living up to his obligations, but they will go and kill their brother or sister to get a vote or prevent a vote.

There are already qualified women serving in our government—Babsy Grange is a strong JLP member; Beverly Manley is another powerful force who I believe worked well with Michael Manley when he was prime minister, and that's the PNP side. There's also Portia Simpson, who could be the next prime minister, because she's very strong. Each time I see her, I say, "Sister Portia, please be the one to ease the pain!" People still look for the good woman behind every strong man. We need to bring that good woman forward, especially in Jamaica, where we have been so far behind. Women do have a very strong authority that is not being used. They're meant to be leaders also; government is not just a man's job. It's important for us to move that good woman from behind to beside—and sometimes in front!

As for me, these days I just want to be myself. People ask: "Why do you still go to the market every Friday or Saturday at 6 A.M.? You don't have to go to the market, send the helper!" No—I don't think so! I'm glad to have the time to be able to do that now, to do what I love to do. My friends at the market enjoy seeing me; I sometimes shoot videos there with everybody singing and dancing.

Even at this age, things are still unfolding, life and work continue to open up for me. Trying new things is as important as carrying on. About eight years ago an American lecture bureau contacted me—there had been some requests for me to speak about the life of Bob Marley during Black History Month. For a few years, with my girlfriends Dahima and Eleanor Wint, and with Errol Barrett to assist us, I traveled to various American universities where we spoke about Bob, showed pictures, and held question-and-answer sessions not only about Bob's life but about Rastafari and Africa. I got so relaxed and well into this that I looked forward to every Black History Month—until I found that I was talking more than singing and began to wonder whether I'd lost some of my vocal range because I hadn't been taking time for any vocal training. I had to ask myself, where am I going? But the students came out to the lectures—whole classes even attended—and the record company was pleased because they then wanted to hear more of Bob Marley's music and went out and bought it. So this was an incentive, to know that the love was still there.

The students' favorite part of my speech was the story about Bob coming through the window of Aunty's house—it would bring laughter and "Oooh!" and "Oh no!" And after, during the questions, there was more about "What did Aunty do?" and "How did you and Bob feel about that? Were you upset for a long time after? I know, I know!" These were young people's questions, because they're about the same age as we were then and doing the same things. So it was fun for them to know that Bob and Rita also did that. It humanizes, makes the superstar a real person, just a normal human being with a special mission. And knowing Bob, he would have liked that too. That was him—for him, the sympathy was most important, this is what made him what he was, this was what he cherished.

Looking closely at myself, regarding myself as a person who needs my attention, has now become a priority. You live long enough and inevitably you reach a point where you realize you have to take care of yourself as well as you take care of everyone else. Being a Leo, I tend to really go heart out for other people and their needs, to overlook myself because I feel I have the handle, but that's when you get cut by the blade. Some people think that because you have the handle you've got the whole—but that's not all of it. You can get lost in *every day every day,* and you think you're supposed to. Because you have the handle; you've always done that, and that's what you have to do. And you'll just keep on doing doing doing—and only at the end of the day will you remember, wow, I didn't take time out to meditate . . .

The one thing I almost forget to do is to take care of me, because right now I'm diabetic, all because of the stress of working, bad eating habits, sometimes not being able to eat what you're supposed to, because you have a meeting or you're on the phone and so you miss lunch, or your next meeting is right at lunchtime. Until the doctors announce: high blood pressure, diabetes, watch out . . .

And then here comes menopause—for laughs! I can understand why they call it men-o-pause. It may really put you on pause where masculine relationships are concerned. You may find you're not the same girl, you may even lose your zeal and your want for lovemaking, though it could be the men who really step back—*they* pause! They pause if you're not so attracted to sex anymore, they pause when your hot flashes become miserable, and *aaarggh*—you don't want to see *nobody* today!

But life continues and I still sometimes want to be loved. Though after you've been there and done that, and know this and know that, you may want to take a break. Faced with this new life, new touch—touch me somewhere else, baby, that feels good—you realize you still have feelings. If you have a partner who really loves you, there are moments you can cherish, without anything to prove—you don't have to prove you can do it because you've done it! All this is why I'm saying I really need to look out for me now. Because here I'm looking at grown children and grandchildren, who want to keep me active: "Grandma, you have to take us there, we have to go do this, we have to do that!" And I'm certainly not going to give up!

I didn't start singing publicly again right after Bob passed, I *couldn't* have, I'd have gone crazy. I couldn't leave the work of the foundation. There was no way I would have walked away from it. I had to stand up for his rights—our rights—and defend them, pursue them, and carry them on.

Still, even though I was mainly doing that, if I hadn't kept up with a little bit of my singing career, I'd have gone even crazier. At the studio people were always so encouraging: "Mrs. Marley, please remember, you can stay here and do one song, and when you get time you can come in and do another." So I was nipping little by little, until finally I said, "Look at this, here's ten songs, let's put out an album." On it were songs I cowrote with Bob, some that other people wrote for me or that were cowritten.

Also, people were always saying, hey, you should do a concert. And so gradually I found time to do this, and was inspired to keep on. Added to this was the fact that I started going all over the world for one reason or another—even just to meet lawyers to sign agreements—and was asked when I'd be available to do a show.

The first time I went out as a solo was with the Fab Five Band. When I went onstage—this was long after Bob's funeral—and the light was on me alone, I couldn't help thinking, "Here I am again!" I had been pursued by Fab Five's drummer, Grub Cooper, who was my musical director and has worked with the family for years as our vocal director for albums. When it comes to recordings, he does vocals, very specifically—and he writes, he's the writer of my first big hit, "One Draw," which became international and was one of the first 12-inch reggae records to enter the *Billboard* charts in America.

That first solo flight after such a long break was a sign, a moment of "Oh my god, I'm really gonna *do* it!" Ever since—and that was a while ago—I've taken my measure from that moment. Because when the light is on you, and you're on that stage, and they're clapping, you know it's still happening. Sometimes I've said to myself, hey, it's unbelievable that I still have the strength. When I was forty I thought that when I reached fifty I wouldn't be able to go on performing, but then fifty came and went and I'm still at it. Just ready. And with my focus on giving, it's good to receive too, to accept that standing ovation and that smile.

My fourth album, *We Must Carry On,* which was released in 1991, became a best-seller and was nominated for a Grammy award (you have to be a best-seller even to be considered for nomination, which I like because it really means that people are playing your music). So that gave me a push to tell myself, as the song says, "We must carry on, *you* must carry on." To me it meant take the time for your career because you still have work to do. Carry on.

I still tour, though not for long periods, because now I feel I must spend time with those thirty-eight grandchildren. Though I think they'd prefer to go on tour with me: "Grandma, I can play your drums!" or "I can sing with you, Grandma, I could be an I-Three!" I think they're very well musically inclined. Still, I adjust my schedule for them. When I do travel, it's often with some of the old crew from the days of being on the road with Bob. It feels good to work with some members of the Wailers. I think that's important—as people say, sometimes it's best to stick with the evil you know! And as Bob sings, "In this great future, we can't forget the past."

I like touring for the fun of it, for getting up there and jigalooing— although I find I'm not jigalooing as much as I used to, because I've put on some extra pounds that I didn't have when I was able to jig around! I'm fearing—oh my gosh, see fat me still jigging around onstage! But I hate to stand still onstage, I *can't* stand still! Because when the music hits you, you're feeling no pain!

My most recent album is called *Sunshine After Rain*. I guess the writers figured it was time I started singing about love again, time for me to bring back that love to my voice. Sometimes it seems as if I was work-driven for so long, just like so many wives and mothers in the entertainment business, trying to ensure that their husbands and children understand that all that glitters is not gold.

I've always had a hand in writing, and I'm really looking forward to writing or cowriting more songs, sharing my feelings with millions of women, millions of sisters. Lots of times women tell me, "Rita, if I hadn't listened to you, I don't know what I'd have done" or "Rita, your song helped me get through this" or even "Your music made me decide *not* to do this!" Even when I perform a song written by someone else, I have to put myself in it and change this word to that, just to be sure I relate to it, that I feel it. I don't sing a song just because it's bouncy or because it has a swing. I sing it because the words mean something, to me and to many other people.

That very first album I did after Bob passed was the hardest. It was like getting over everything that happened. Most of the songs on that recording session are there because I allowed myself to sing, and Grub Cooper had said to do an album but take it slow, one song at a time. "Do some of your old songs," he suggested. "Do some of Bob's songs. Do the songs you actually love." Because I hadn't been able to express my hurt, my grief. Everything had been deflected into work, too much work to think. Every day it was, you can't grieve now. You can't grieve now, you have to wake up feeling strong to have this meeting. You can't grieve now, you have to fly here to meet with the lawyers. You can't grieve now, we have a meeting in New York with the administrators. My grieving was always "can't now, can't now." So Grub said, "You know the best way to express your grief—or you're going to go crazy—is to sing. Sing!"

I thought, wow, that's exactly what Bob said, his last words to me just before he passed. And, prophet that he was, he must have seen the future when he wrote "No Woman No Cry." He must have known he'd have to "push on through." But he also must have known that when he was gone, everything was "gonna be all right." So I started to sing, as he told me to do, and just as he said it would be, everything was all right. And I'm still singing, and it still is. All right! Rastafari!